Bob Burton

BAIL ENFORCER

The Advanced Bounty Hunter

PALADIN PRESS
BOULDER, COLORADO

Also by Bob Burton:

Bounty Hunter

Bail Enforcer:
The Advanced Bounty Hunter
by Bob Burton

ISBN 0-87364-578-2
Printed in the United States of America

Published by Paladin Press, a division of
Paladin Enterprises, Inc., P.O. Box 1307,
Boulder, Colorado 80306, USA.
(303) 443-7250

Direct inquiries and/or orders to the above address.

Author photo by Volker Corell Photography

Neither the author nor the publisher assumes
any responsibility for the use or misuse of
information contained in this book.

“There is no hunting like the hunting of man, and those who have hunted armed men long enough and liked it, never care for anything else thereafter.”

Ernest Hemingway

Contents

Preface

In my first book, *Bounty Hunter,* I tried to spell out for the beginning bounty hunter some of the laws that pertain to this profession, the historical background, some tradecraft, and how to deal with other elements within the business, such as law-enforcement officials, bail bondsmen, and courts. Within the confines of that book, where my intention was to give an overview of the profession, I was unable to dwell on the "meat and potatoes" of bail enforcement, only the "how to."

Bail Enforcer is designed to inform, in the most complete fashion yet published, how to get the contract; track, find, and arrest the defendant; and deal with fugitive detail officers, courts, bondsmen (and women), snitches, and people who will get in your way.

This volume will help you achieve status as a member of that most unique community: the American bounty hunter. I use a step-by-step process that will enable you to restudy and rethink everything you do and are instructed to do.

Appendix D includes forms that you can photocopy. These forms will help you become more organized, professional, and most importantly, more efficient as a bail enforcement agent.

I hope this book answers most of your questions and then some. If it doesn't, there is a list of additional reading in Appendix F.

The bottom line is that this book is meant to be *studied*, not just read. You must reread it as you would any other career guide.

You are holding in your hands the most complete and thorough book ever published on bounty hunting. Use it the way it was intended to be used and you will be on your way to an exciting, rewarding, and action-packed career.

Good luck.

Bob Burton
Santa Barbara, California

Acknowledgments

In the course of writing a book, one has to rely on the judgment, advice, information, and counsel offered and asked of friends, peers, and total strangers. This book is no exception to that practice. I am indebted to the following individuals for their time given to me—in many cases, as a total stranger—in answering questions and digging up forms and other items to complete this book.

To Suzy Denno of the FBI, I am very appreciative for wading through paperwork and other people's delay in getting me information on the National Crime Information Center (NCIC) and the *FBI Law Enforcement Bulletin* on bail-bond arrest.

Thanks to former U.S. Attorney General Edwin Meese, now with the Heritage Foundation in Washington, D.C., who steered me in the right direction and gave me the right "names" to open doors to further research, which saved me much time. Mr. Meese and I were solicited for public comment on the bounty placed on General Manuel Noriega of Panama. As such, we both had an opinion on bounty-incentive arrest/capture, and I enjoyed hearing Mr. Meese's thoughts on the subject.

Much help came from working bounty hunters who have collected legal opinions as a course of business. Foremost are Dan Cuellar of Fresno, California; Maurice Jones, Chief, Recovery Division, ProBailUS, Las Vegas, Nevada; and Lance Wilkinson of Manchester, New Hampshire. Special thanks to Ray Hawkins of Nipomo, California. Ray is one of the old-time California bounty hunters who has amassed a wealth of bail arrest cases. He generously shared them all with me for the writing of this book.

Special thanks must go to William Bryson of the Solicitor General's Office, U.S. Department of Justice, for his helpful and instructive advice on pursuing some of the filings and briefs that were used in this book.

And a wealth of thanks and gratitude to Sgt. Bob Casey, Commander, Fugitive Detail, Santa Barbara, California Sheriff's Office, for many hours of patient and time-consuming advice on the criminal justice computer network, and his ability to always put me in contact with the right person throughout the country.

CHAPTER ONE

What's in a Name?

Outside of the trade, those in my business are called "bounty hunters." It's an old and colorful title full of myth, legend, and hard reality. Most people think of the "Old West" when they hear the term, but reality has it that there were damn few bounty hunters then. Lack of communication was a major obstacle to being a successful bounty hunter, as was the slowness of travel. Bail bondsmen were a rare breed in the small towns of the nineteenth-century West and South. Casino owners, ranchers, and the other wealthy friends of the arrested person would post "bail," which was often nothing more than the word of the bailor ("I'll see that Jeth is there for the trial, Sheriff.").

The fact is that there are many more bounty hunters today than yesteryear. Due to modern communication, quickness of travel, and a more systematic method of exchanging information, recovery work is now a more viable business.

Despite the public's desire to call us "bounty hunter," we in the trade often refer to ourselves as "recovery agents," or "bail enforcement agents." What you choose to call yourself may affect how much business you get. Some bondsmen tend to look at those who call themselves bounty hunters as new to the game. In conversation, however, we refer to ourselves as bounty hunter, or even "hunter." It's shorter and easier for discussion's sake.

The national association that bounty hunters belong to for professional networking is the National Association of Bail Enforcement Agents. As the trade becomes more needful of professionalization, I suspect even the name of the game itself will change to something such as "bail enforcement" rather than bounty hunting.

As you progress in this business and develop less of an attitude of a bounty hunter and more of one as a bail enforcement agent, so too will your demeanor change. You soon will find yourself more accepted on a professional level with the people you will be working with. This includes lawyers, licensed private investigators, surety company executives, judges, and so on. All of these individuals will be inclined to not take you seriously if you present a card along the lines of, "John Doe, Bounty Hunter—Anyplace, Anywhere, Anytime. Danger no problem."

The following is an example of a clear and effective card that turns up more often than not from the bounty hunters I meet. Everybody in the trade will know exactly what you do when they see this card, and it offers comfort to the more structured and conventional types that you will *always* (unfortunately) run into.

With many years of television and movies coloring the business, you have a lot to live down, bring up, and push aside. Professionalize yourself immediately and you will find the trade to be very productive. The following chapters give more detail and offer direct advice on how to achieve this.

Owner Midwest Bail Recovery		Member: NABEA
	John Smith Bail Enforcement Agent	
Phone #: (112) 345-6789 101-2345		123 Main Street Des Moines, Iowa

CHAPTER TWO

On Clothing

The simple fact of how you are dressed will often determine if you get your fugitive or not. It might also decide if you get hurt or even killed in the process of arrest.

Because bounty hunting will keep one in a vehicle or behind a desk for unusually lengthy periods of time, most of us dress for comfort. (In fact, our profession can be more sedentary than a gardener's.) Yet sometimes comfortable clothing can lead to injury.

For example, many times when I am making an arrest, I appear more disheveled and unkempt than the fugitive. I don't like this, but it sometimes is necessary. The fear I have is this: what if there is a struggle and a police unit comes along? If I am holding a firearm, who will the police officer zero in on first? You got it—the disheveled and unkempt guy with the gun. And maybe he will shoot first and *then* ask questions. This scenario has actually arisen with me, and only because I was known was a tragedy averted.

The photographs in this book show several examples of clothing styles than can be worn, including an emerging style called "ID rags."

A police officer coming on to this scene would instantly recognize the man holding the shotgun (in this case, Dan Cuellar) as a bounty hunter. (Photo by John Taylor)

In choosing clothing, you always have to consider the fugitive's mind-set. Most fugitives are looking for detectives looking for them. And what do detectives wear? Suits. I'm not talking about a detective on an undercover operation or a narc, but an ordinary detective who would usually wear a suit, maybe with an open collar, depending on department policy, weather, and locale.

The fugitive is also on the lookout for uniformed officers who can get him only if they stop him for a routine traffic violation or recognize him on the sidewalk, knowing there is a warrant for his arrest. Yet uniformed officers don't usually do formal investigations per se. They handle traffic accidents and shooting scenes on arrival, but they generally turn it over to the Detective Bureau after the report is made.

So by knowing your man's (or woman's) way of thinking, you will be able to sidle up to him wearing your Harley-Davidson shirt or brown shirt with the "Parcel Service" patches and inform him, while he's playing pool, that he is under arrest.

One of the better hunters in California is Dan Cuellar of Fresno. Dan is a hulking, middle-aged man with a brilliant mind and an absolutely smooth conversational ability. He is mature, knowledgeable, and successful at what he does. And he does it with hair well past his shoulders. This "look" allows Dan to sidle right up to his targets and pin them against a wall before they realize he is not "one of them."

The downside of this look is a sometimes hostile reception from law-enforcement authorities. Dan is well known and respected in his own area, but, like the rest of us, he sometimes has to travel to other counties or states. Oftentimes the law-enforcement people in these areas *do not* like out-of-town or out-of-state bounty hunters coming in and arresting their own people, even criminals. Fortunately, this mentality is not widespread.

Dan's trade-off is to get the bad guy and then work his way through any obstacles thrown up by closed-minded individuals. Others without his moxie, skill, and experience would be advised to maintain an appearance in keeping with the business they are a representative of and the authorities they have to deal with, and yet not stand out while looking for the fugitive.

In short, a compromise should be met that satisfies your need for safety, a professional appearance, and a sort of "camouflage" that will enable you to get close to the bad guy.

When choosing the right clothes, you also have to consider the fugitive's neighborhood. If he lives in a scummy neighborhood, don't sit in a car or be seen too often wearing a shirt and tie or you will stand out as a possible detective. Yet it would be perfectly proper and safe to walk into the suspect's workplace and arrest him or her while wearing a business suit (which I tend to do) to make it more professional. This is especially so if you are out of state and in a jurisdiction that does not authorize bounty hunting, such as Oregon or Illinois. It assures the fugitive's co-workers that all is in order so they won't call the coppers on you. The subject also will think it's legal and will therefore be less likely to resist.

In fact, it is not unusual to have a prisoner taken away from you and released by a police officer who is not aware of a bounty hunter's legal right to arrest. The right appearance and demeanor can go a long way in defusing the situation. Therefore, do not wear camouflaged military clothing, combat boots, studded leather jackets, unwashed clothes, or clothing proclaiming you as a "Bounty Hunter."

Along the same line, do not bring guns into a courtroom or do anything that will make you enemies among the legal and law-enforcement community *that you have to work with*. It is very important to realize that the more ability you have to work smoothly within this group, the easier your job will be. The net result will be a high recovery rate and a thick wallet.

Clothing can "make the man," as the saying goes. If you are busting through the front door of a house with guns waving in a nonsubterfuge raid, then a jacket with "Bail Enforcement Agent" written clearly on it would be the most appropriate attire. Don't think that the bad guy won't shoot in a heartbeat if he thinks you are from a rival gang or have been hired to work him over. But if he sees that jacket and ID, he will hesitate to shoot, realizing that he doesn't need additional charges to his original petty theft, drunk driving, or dope-selling charge. Also, any police arriving on the scene can quickly differentiate between bad guy and good guy, a job they have to do instantaneously on arrival. If you are wearing or holding a gun, the ID jacket makes the whole scene more understandable to the police. This is not to say that you won't be drawn down on for safety's sake, but it is less likely to happen.

The purpose of the ID jacket is to add formality and professionalism to the scene. You have probably seen groups of men rushing into a house on television true-crime shows. What are most prominent are the large labels on their backs that read DEA AGENT, POLICE, MARSHAL, and others. I can't remember ever having seen this scene with guys rushing in wearing T-shirts with no identifiers.

Bearing in mind that a bail enforcement agent is essentially an insurance investigator with the authority to arrest, take a lesson from the officers on those programs and think safety, professionalism, and authority. After all, the clothing you appear in and your manner are sometimes the only authority that will enable you to succeed. And one does not get a second chance to make a first impression.

CHAPTER THREE

Some Thoughts for the Beginner

Despite all the romantic nonsense that a lot of people have in their heads about bounty hunting, it is a profession with all the attendant legal and civil nuances one finds in any business or trade today.

In approaching a bail-bond agent for a contract, the most important thing to consider is the initial appearance you make. That first appearance may be the *only* appearance you will get if it isn't a good one. Remember, why should a bail-bond agent jeopardize his business by giving a contract to a total stranger and risking a wrongful arrest or even a shooting of the fugitive? The bondsman will look at you with the same questioning eyes he reserves for his bail-bond applicants. He is a shrewd judge of character, a bit cynical (and rightfully so), questions everything, and hopefully is a good businessman or woman who intends to stay in business.

Obviously, you do not want to stand in front of him with a résumé stating how many weapons systems you can handle, how much weight you can lift, and that you are a black belt in karate. The bonds agent does not want to hear this. The prisoner must be brought back alive.

When approaching a bondsman for the first time, even if you are a long-time recovery agent, dress accordingly. Neat clothing is a must to make a good first impression. What comes out of your mouth after that will depend on how well you studied this book and prepared yourself.

A major part of your preparation is to draw up a list of friends and associates who work for the following:

- Telephone company.
- Electric company.
- Gas company.
- Post office.
- Social services (welfare, etc.).
- Police department.
- Sheriff's department.
- Other law-enforcement agencies.
- Any agencies, public or private, that have lists of people's names, addresses, and/or phone numbers.

This list could be virtually endless. It is the beginning of your network of assets that will help you find someone. If you are not able to access these lists personally, your friends or friendly contacts will do it for you. It may cost you $20 or $120, but that's the cost of doing business.

Having this list of assets will enable you to talk intelligently to the bonds agent for the first time. An experienced bounty hunter will be able to "bailspeak" with the bondsman and develop a certain amount of trust immediately or shortly thereafter. But again, dressing nicely is imperative. I don't necessarily mean a suit, but I don't suggest a black Harley Davidson T-shirt either.

The chances of the bonds agent offering you a juicy case right off are slim. If he does offer you a case, it will more likely be an old one he has written off as uncatchable.

A wise novice bounty hunter would offer to work for nothing alongside the agency's existing recovery agent. Remember, before you arrived on the scene, the bondsman had already discovered a bounty hunter he could trust to arrest the fugitive in a sane and judicial fashion and deliver him to jail, with little or no physical injury. These are civil and criminal prisoners, not prisoners of war.

You might stress your ability to pump the telephone or gas company through your connections. Or that you have been a long-time resident of the town and are willing to learn the trade by apprenticing yourself to an experienced bounty hunter. The hunter most likely won't even be in the office when you go there, and the bondsman probably will not give you his phone number. He may, however, take yours with the promise of passing it on.

The bounty hunter, if he has been around awhile, has been approached dozens of times by "wannabes." Most hunters keep a sort of "resource file," a book cross referenced by state, city, and even by public utility listing names of individuals that the hunter has had contact with and considers to be potential helpers and assistants. Should the hunter call you, be prepared to offer reasons why he should hire you.

The hunter's first inclination will be to ask physical questions like how you look, how big you are, and, most importantly, how smart you are. This is a business of individuals that could talk their way into Iran while dressed as a rabbi. The ability to think fast on your feet in both passive and dangerous situations is a must. If you are a fast thinker and a slow talker, so be it. Chances are the hunter will recognize that and note approvingly. But you had *at least* better know such basics as where the county courthouse or city hall is, and certainly the county jail.

Before approaching a bondsman or hunter, find out about the details of the bail-bond industry, including the different types of bail-bond arrests, where the prisoner should be taken, and so on. And before going any further, you had best know what laws govern bounty hunting in your state and even adjoining states. This information can be found in my earlier book, *Bounty Hunter*, or by looking at the penal or criminal codes. Look under Bail Arrest, Surrender by Surety, Bail, or any combination of those titles.

This is the *minimum* amount of information that you should be armed with before talking with a bonds agent or hunter. As you can see, there's much more to it than simply finding a skip and convincing that person to come with you. Information is your most important weapon in this business.

If you live in a small town, the bounty hunter might be familiar with you or at least your family name. And if so inclined, he may share with you a name that he is looking for. If he does, consider it your first building block and no more. You won't have any arrest authority until the bail bondsman gives it to you, but you may get your chance to look for someone.

Should the bounty hunter take you in, expect to work for nothing or, at most, twenty to fifty dollars. Remember, he is a businessman—why should he train the competition? But being a bounty hunter and hunting bounty are two different things. To bounty hunters, full-time pros, anyone with less than fifty arrests would be considered a beginner.

Instead of passing your name on to the hunter, the bonds agent may just wish to use you for an office "gofer" or errand runner. Do it. After all, you have nothing else to offer except your labor and an eager mind. In the process you will learn about the bail industry and how to arrest those that fail to make their bail appearances.

Be aware that many bonds agents make their own arrests. They themselves are both the bondsman and bounty hunter. As bondsmen get older, too busy, or move into other businesses, however, they will assign these bail skips to someone . . . and it may be you.

CHAPTER FOUR

The Arrest Contract

The business of being a bounty hunter is simply to find, arrest, and book into jail a subject who fails to make his or her ordered court appearance and places in jeopardy the posted bail bond.

That bail bond was posted by a bail-bond agent to secure the freedom of the arrested subject. In the bail-bond contract are clauses that demand that the subject abide by all court orders and appointments or be subjected to arrest (or "surrender"; the two terms are used interchangably) by the bail-bond agent. It is essentially a civil contract in which one party may arrest the other and hand him over to the lawful authorities if the second party fails to perform as the contract stipulates. It is a unique contract that is perfectly legal and performs a social good.

The bail-bond contract usually states that any costs that the bondsman incurs in finding and surrendering the subject to the authorities may be assessed against that individual or the collateral he used to secure the bail bond. While these contractual rights may vary from state to state, the basic tenet holds true: jump bail, go back to jail!

A bail bond can be likened to a loan: if the applicant (the jailed person) has no collateral, such as a car, motorcycle, home, job, or savings, then someone else must cover the amount of the bail. This practice goes back to the early days of bail, when it wasn't unusual to find pigs, chickens, or a treasured cow put up as collateral. In fact, one can still find this sort of thing posted in some areas of the country.

More commonly, a cash bail is posted as collateral, or cash and a house or two, especially in drug arrests involving big bail amounts. It might even be a signed MasterCard charge form that the bondsman can use later in case things go sour. (Some areas disallow a credit card, as it gives an advantage to "well-off" people who are more likely to have one.) Each state has its own attitude and laws governing bail collateral, and it's something that all bounty hunters should be familiar with.

In most states, the subject does not have to necessarily jump bail in order to be arrested. If the bail-bond agent fears or hears that the subject is about to flee to another state or Mexico, he may have him arrested. Another reason for arrest would be if the person who has put up the collateral for bail changes his mind and wishes to "get off" the bail. At that point, the bondsman usually has no choice but to arrest the subject until new collateral is posted.

In one case I encountered, a well-to-do woman covered a $10,000 bail for a slimy, snot-nosed druggie. She put up her savings as collateral. About two weeks later, after he had made a court appearance, she decided she wanted out of the bail bond. The bondsman had no choice but to have the defendant arrested. He called me up and informed me of the situation. Since the contract she signed stipulated that she would cover all recovery costs, I contacted her and informed her of the fee. She agreed and signed an Indemnitor Order of Surrender form (see Appendix D).

I arrested the defendant, much to his chagrin. He had, after all, obeyed all the laws after his arrest and was bewildered as to why she had backed off. Lo and behold, he called her after I booked him and she bailed him out again for the same amount! Three weeks later the same bondsman called me, laughing, and informed me that she wanted him arrested again. I wasn't happy with the situation, but money is money.

Having a second form signed, I arrested and booked the defendant. By now my sympathy was sliding toward him and away from her. She was simply a bleeding-heart liberal with a bunch of second thoughts. The part of this that is hard to believe is it was repeated a *third* time, only with a different bondsman. The first one didn't wish to go through it again, as it was distasteful and the courts don't like this sort of thing. The third time was not unlike the first two. She had a change of heart and the second bondsman had him surrendered in court when he came to make his appearance. It was the most unusual case of its kind I had run into, and while profitable, was not the kind of case that offered any satisfaction, social or professional.

The most common reason for arrest is that the subject "skipped." This is a loose term that generally means that rather than face a hearing, trial, and perhaps eventual prosecution, the applicant decides to "skip" his or her court appearance.

At this point a clock starts ticking, a very expensive clock. From the day the subject fails to appear, which is called "bail forfeiture," the bonds agent has a certain period of time to find him. If he does not find the fugitive in that time, he must pay, usually by cashier's check, the posted amount of the bail. A $5,000 or $8,000 or more bail can put a big dent in any business, including a bondsman's. (See Appendix D for a copy of the letter used by one court in California to notify a bondsman of a forfeiture.)

Another reason that the bondsman may want a person found could be personal or for business reasons. For instance, after bailing someone out of jail, the bondsman expects the subject to stop by the bonding office to sign papers, pay some more on the bond (the premium on a bond is usually 10 percent), or bring forward more collateral.

Bear in mind that the bondsman often meets the subject for the first time (*if* he even meets him) at maybe three in the morning. Since the subject cannot usually come out of jail and sign papers, a meeting is arranged by a loved one, spouse, or friend. Usually this contracting party will call the bondsman and inform him of the arrest. At that point the bondsman will call the jail to find out the bail amount, the charges, and what the detained person is all about. He will do a quick computer scan to see if the detained person has been a "customer" before and then, in all likelihood, go over and post the bail bond.

The next morning the bondsman expects everyone involved to be in his office to finish up the deal. Yet the ex-prisoner might not rush into the office the next day, earning the immediate distrust of the bondsman. A bad start. Another bad sign is if, in the early morning's glare, the collateral is not what was promised over the phone; for instance, if the 1987 BMW sedan turns out to be a BMW motorcycle. It's still worth a bit, but not enough to cover the $10,000 bail. The bondsman is getting nervous and no one is returning his calls.

Usually the bondsman will take a day or two of this, maybe even a week if the bail and his commission are big enough, before deciding it was a bad deal. At this point he has no collateral and the exposure of a $10,000 bail walking around. He wants the subject arrested! The police won't do anything since it's strictly a civil law problem. Remember, the subject's first court appearance is still twenty days away and he hasn't "failed to appear" yet. The bondsman won't give him that chance.

In this scenario, the bondsman will ask the bounty hunter to arrest the skip. Usually the skip does not yet have a fugitive mentality and will answer the phone at his house. The arrest could be as simple as calling him up and telling him that he paid too much for the bond premium and that you have a refund for him. In order to preclude the statement "just mail it to me," say that, like everything in this industry, it's in cash, so you will need a receipt. You will be at the Acme Restaurant down the street at 1:00 P.M. for lunch; why not meet there for coffee (and handcuffs).

When a genuine "Failure To Appear" (FTA) situation is encountered, all effort must be exerted to find the skip immediately. Yet all your paperwork must be in order to enable you, as the bounty hunter, to exonerate the bail-bond agent. The key word here is *exonerate.* Exoneration is a legal term meaning that the bail-bond agent has been freed of any obligation to pay the forfeited bail bond. This is most often accomplished by surrendering the bail-bond fugitive to the court of jurisdiction or the court having the original authority in the case. This is where you come in, and it is the sole reason that you are working for the bail bondsman. Sure, you are in it to make money for your efforts. But one thing that will always follow you is your reputation. Like any profession, you want people to say that you were *professional, timely,* and *legal*—all vital traits in this business.

You will need several pieces of paperwork regarding the subject in question. Foremost will be a copy of the bail-bond agreement from the bondsman. This bail-bond agreement will have some basic information about the fugitive that you will need. Usually this information came from a third person—the collateral—and was filled out leaning against a wall at the county jail. It's not always neat, but it's still valuable. Sometimes the information is false or mistaken, but it is something to begin with and often is all you will have to go on.

You will also be given an "Authority to Arrest" form (see Appendix D) that should be filled out by the bondsman. Most states require this form when surrendering the bad guy to jail. In reality, I have only been asked about it twenty to thirty times. Most jailers know nothing of it. Some states say the form should be notarized, but that has rarely arisen with me either. Nonetheless, it is nice to have when transporting the subject should you be stopped by a police unit who wants to know why you have a handcuffed prisoner.

So now you have a copy of the bail-bond agreement and the form authorizing arrest. Another important document is a certified copy of the bail bond that was posted with the jail that originally held the bad guy. This can be obtained from the court clerk who handled the case. Generally, a municipal court handles misdemeanors and a county or superior court handles felonies. The court clerk will issue you a certified copy of the bail for either no cost or seven to ten dollars. This certified copy must be on your person when surrendering the prisoner.

Usually when a bail bond is forfeited, the court will issue a bench warrant. This means that, in theory, while you are looking for the bail skip, so is the local sheriff's "fugitive detail." This group will become a major asset that you must court and at the same time assist. Every time you arrest someone, it is one less case for them to deal with. In some areas, the city police have their own fugitive detail, and they as well as the sheriff will be looking for the skip. Sometimes a BOL (Be On the Lookout) for the fugitive will be issued to all patrol units, but this rarely happens unless it was a well-publicized crime.

Armed with the bail-bond agreement, the certified copy of the bail, and the arrest-authorization form, make an appointment to see the head of the fugitive detail. Often, this "detail" is only one man in a county sheriff's department. If you present yourself in a manner that he is used to seeing others in his business—that is, neatly groomed and dressed—he will most likely cooperate with you.

What you would like from the fugitive officer is a copy of the booking slip and possibly a photo of the subject. The photo is often the easiest to get. Pictures are sometimes released to the media and are not protected as thoroughly under the Privacy Act as is the information on the booking slip. If you can't obtain the information you want through friendly cooperation, most states will issue court orders that allow you to first request and then sue to get government data. This includes criminal information. I have found, however, and so will you, that trust and honey will get you a lot farther in this business.

Cooperation between yourself and the fugitive officer should be a two-way street. Every chance you get, pass on information that is helpful to him; he will grow to trust you and eventually go out of his way to help. He also eats lunch everyday . . .

Now you are armed with the right paperwork from the bondsman, the court clerk, and, hopefully, the fugitive detail. This information should be placed in a letter- or legal-sized file folder. I use letter size because most of the documents I handle fit this size file, and it is simply less cumbersome than legal.

I often carry all information in a size-14 Kraft brown envelope, which is capable of handling *any* folded document. The forms must be carefully treated, as they are, after all, legal documents. Yet in any case, all documents must be checked and rechecked to make sure all numbers and data jibe. Therefore, you can transfer the data on the booking slip to the outside of the envelope so a quick glance will give the most pertinent information while saving wear and tear on the documents.

You are now ready to go to work.

CHAPTER FIVE

The Basics

The first item of business is to confirm the fugitive's name. Is the name shown on the booking slip or bail-bond agreement his legal name or an alias?

This can be done by checking his car registration and driver's license. Most motor vehicle departments have a standard procedure for getting the information you require. Ironically, even if you are chasing John Doe and he is really John Smith, it matters not. As long as everybody knows him as Doe, they will steer you to your man under the name they know. Fortunately, this problem will not arise often enough to make it a major concern.

Begin to compile all the information you develop on a work sheet (see Appendix D). This should always be attached to your paperwork as the first sheet showing.

All the information you gather is important, even if it seems meaningless at the time you acquire it. As one of the more literate investigators in this country has said: "All investigations have a life of their own. You never know what piece is the last piece of the jigsaw puzzle until you are on your fugitive, sometimes almost in surprise. Thus, all information is important from the start."

MAKING VISITS

Starting with the address on the bail-bond application and those addresses of his or her relatives, loved ones, and employer, begin making visits. While doing so, *always* be prepared for a surprise confrontation with the fugitive. You should keep handcuffs on your person at all times, and be ready to make an arrest.

Don't forget to check with the neighbors on either side of the homes you visit. In fact, it's usually a good idea to go there first. I tell these people frankly that I am looking for a fugitive. Most folks don't like to have a fugitive visiting next door and will volunteer information quite readily. Sometimes you have to refer to the fugitive as the "loudmouth in the red car with loud mufflers." If the subject is true to form, the neighbors will generally have him or her earmarked for destruction long before you arrived. Armed with generally objective information provided by the neighbors, your visit to a loved one or relative will be in better perspective.

If none of the addresses on the bail-bond agreement are correct, then you can assume fraud and a predisposition to skip. Should this happen, you will have to go to public sources.

TELEPHONE

Sometimes it is as simple as calling directory assistance. Often the fugitive will have the phone listed in his wife's name, so don't overlook asking for her name, too. If the phone number but no street address is given, the prefix will tell you what part of town he lives in. The prefix is the first three digits of the number (not the area code).

If you do get the phone number but no address, another method is to call during the day and talk to the wife, should she be home, or, even better, a school-age child. The conversation should go this way:

You: "Hello, Mrs. Doe?"
Her: "Yes."

You: "This is Operator 35 in billing with the telephone company. We are getting your bills back and I know you don't want your phone turned off. What is your correct billing address?"

Her: "Oh gosh, really? What went wrong? What number do you have?"

You: "We have 123 Main Street, this city." (You will have to give a more realistic number and street and provide the city.)

Her: "Well, our bills are usually sent to this address. I don't know how you got that address."

A lot of people simply say "this address," assuming that you, the telephone operator, know what that address is. You will have to dig a bit more, but it's easy:

You: "Well, Mrs. Doe, what *is* your current address so we can send a bill to your residence?"

You can purchase a cassette tape that plays the sounds of a business office. Simply play it in the background. The sounds of a telephone company's business office in the background will add credibility to your performance.

POST OFFICE

If the address on the application is no good, see if there is a forwarding address. Maybe that supposedly false address was in fact a good address at one time. Mail clerks will give you a form to fill out; that and one dollar will get you the new address.

You can also mail a letter to the old address with "DO NOT FORWARD, ADDRESS CORRECTION REQUESTED" on the lower left front of the envelope. The post office will send the letter back to you with the new address handwritten or printed on the envelope.

If the subject is using a post office box, you will have

to go into that post office (or any post office, for that matter) and fill out a form. If the box is used for business, they will tell you the address of the box holder. They are not supposed to tell you if it's for residential or personal use. To get around this, write "Doe Enterprises" in the form's section that asks for the box holder's name. On seeing the commercial name, most clerks will give you the address you need.

Verbally skilled individuals might call the post office in question, ask for the "box section," and say, "This is Hall in the box section at Ventura Main. What address do you have for box-holder 1234?" Generally, a clerk will provide the information to you, a fellow clerk. Do it between 8:30 and 10:00 A.M. Clerks are busy then throwing mail in the boxes and won't hold you up with a bunch of questions. If one does, say an inspector asked you to check it out and you didn't bother to ask him why.

CITY DIRECTORIES

These books are published annually by most cities and moderate-to-large towns. A general trend toward privacy has made city directories more scarce and less effective, yet they are still a good source. Even older books that provide you with an old listing for the fugitive can lead you to past neighbors who may have kept in touch with him. Don't overlook the folks two or three houses away or across the street in your questioning, either.

PUBLIC RECORDS

Many public records are on file that will aid you in compiling a physical description, tracking other individuals in your subject's life, finding old or current addresses and work locations, and leads in general.

Civil records will tell you about your subject's business and personal life. Check under both "Plaintiff" and "Defendant" in the index. This will reveal lawsuits the subject has been involved in, including the names of individuals that have sued or been sued by him. Oftentimes these people will have all sorts of data on the subject, having been in a legal contest with him. You must check out county records held in the county courthouse as well as municipal records usually held in the records center of the lower, city, or municipal court.

CRIMINAL RECORDS

Criminal records will contain a wealth of information regarding contacts and prior crimes, as well as a good physical description of the subject. These records, however, are generally unavailable to the public. You will have to have a contact in the local police agency acquire the information for you. On the other hand, many states have government codes that authorize the release of this information to interested parties. A tip-off: how many times have you seen photographs of wanted people on local television? Lots of times, right? Well, if the police can release information to the media, they can certainly release it to an investigator operating under the same set of state criminal codes.

OTHER RECORDS

Don't overlook marriage and property records as well as auto, boat, motorcycle, and even voter registrations.

Unlike an asset search or background investigation done by a private investigator, you are not gathering facts per se, but rather data that will lead you to an individual. Each piece of data will create a picture of what that person does for a living, what they do every day, and when they do it. Answered questions involving *what*, *when*, and *how* will eventually lead you to the most important answer—*where*?

PEOPLE

Don't overlook people as part of your basic questioning. I have found two types of individuals that pop up as

The author showing a wanted poster to a pizza shop employee. They seem to know what's happening on the streets.

prime sources of information: kids that work in pizza shops and the neighborhood paperboy.

Literally dozens of investigations have been solved by telling a paperboy in a suspect's neighborhood that if he wants to make twenty or fifty dollars to call me if he sees such and such a car at 123 Main Street. I give him my card, tell him I am a bounty hunter, and go home. This saves hours of sitting nearby and possibly getting burned by nosy neighbors. Sure enough, that kid will call and tell you that the car is in the driveway. All you have to do is go to the house or initiate arrangements that you have already worked out to arrest the fugitive. Make damn sure you pay the paperboy what you promised him, and *never* let on to the bad guy how you found out about him.

LABOR UNIONS

Don't overlook the possibility of your man working out of a labor union. Find out what day and time members report for work assignments and then turn up. You can save time by calling to verify that he is a member. Usually they are happy to furnish this information, especially if you state that you only hire "union" and want to make sure John Doe is a member. If he's a member, you will get a prompt affirmation; if not, a very quick negative.

PRETEXTING

Throughout all the contacts you make with governmental and private sources, you will find a need for "pretexting." A pretext is when you obtain information over the phone or face-to-face under false pretenses. Using a ruse to gather information has been a ploy of investigators since the beginning of time.

Over the telephone, a pretext can range from the words actually spoken to the inflection in your voice, anything from authoritative to modest. The basic concept is to *make it easy* for the clerk or holder of information to help you. Even engaging in small talk will break up that clerk's day, and maybe some soft talk will make up for the previous customer who was rude and snotty. Remember, the most complete, expensive, and security-conscious information system is usually guarded and serviced by a minimum-wage employee. I advocate approaching these individuals at 11:45 A.M. when they want to go to lunch, or at 4:45 P.M. when they are about to close up. Usually a clerk or government employee will move the paperwork a bit faster for you at these times.

Success depends on your ability to "smooth talk" someone. This is an art that comes with the job. The investigator's biggest asset is his or her ability to think fast and speak sincerely. I've never met a successful bounty hunter who was not a fast thinker and even faster on his feet. The ability to create scenarios and cover your tracks to prevent compromise of who you are and what you are doing is a lifesaving, fugitive-catching, and money-producing skill.

There are so many available sources to access the fugitive that it is sometimes easy to forget pretexting. In speaking to fellow recovery agents, we all agree that a book on this subject alone would be worth reading once or twice a year. As you progress in this trade, I suggest keeping a loose-leaf or composition-style book with a collection of your own ideas and gimmicks that you have used successfully.

The most powerful weapon a bounty hunter has is a creative and inquiring mind. Never see things as they appear but as what they might be. This applies to what you hear as well.

And most important of all: no rest until the arrest!

CHAPTER SIX

Looking for Judas

Ultimately, your search will lead you to the two stars of this trade: the fugitive and the Judas who betrays him. My belief is that we all have a Judas in our lives. When you find him, whether by luck, deduction, or detective work, your problems are over.

The Judas will, for thirty pieces of silver, tell you exactly where your fugitive is. It may take a while to find this Judas, but when you do, he or she will expect a reward for information. Be prepared to pay it.

My feeling is that out of ten people in anyone's life, three will love him, three will dislike him, and four won't give a damn. The same applies to the fugitive, with perhaps *more* people in the dislike category.

An easy place to begin your search for a Judas is the telephone numbers on the bail-bond agreement. These will usually be numbers for relatives, a husband or wife, friend, employer, or collateral. The FTA worksheet (see Appendix D) is also helpful here.

The first calls you make can go any way. Sometimes the people listed on the application don't know that their friend is now a fugitive and will often steer you right to him. If the skip has a fugitive mind-set, he will have covered his tracks by telling those people what he's up to so they will not cooperate with you. Hence, the hung-up phones.

Somewhere, however, is someone who knows all about your man and will tell you, should you be lucky enough to find him or her. Of course, this person doesn't know you are looking for the fugitive so he or she can't find you. You have to find them.

A record should be made of each call, the time and date you called, and the thrust of the conversation, with a note as to the friendly or hostile nature of the called person. Questions will generally become easier as you get "inside" the skip's personality via the comments of the people called. They will unconsciously offer little hints over the phone that will offer you more and more insight into the fugitive.

You will have to ask questions of a soft and gentle nature. Remember, you are not a policeman, and they have no overwhelming need to cooperate with you. Most of the phoned people will "know their rights."

When calling, I always refer to myself as a bail-bond *worker* in need of getting hold of Mr. Doe. If you are lucky, one of the telephoned individuals will say that he just stepped out for a six pack and will be back in a moment. If so, leave a message for him to call you and beat a path over to that house, if you know the address. This is where a cellular car phone comes in mighty handy.

Eventually, however, word will get out that the bad guy is indeed a bad guy and you are looking for him. At this point you will become an insurance investigator, and technically that is what you are. A bail bond is a form of surety insurance, and you are an insurance investigator with the power to arrest. The term softens the thrust of your questions and is not as offensive as "bounty hunter." I often use this term, especially when speaking to the mother of the fugitive:

> Mrs. Doe, I'm just an insurance investigator; all I want to do is get your boy back into court to take care of this problem. If a rookie cop finds your boy with that warrant over his head, there's no telling what that rookie will do. Why don't you tell me where he is?

Parents hate to be told that their son or daughter is now a fugitive and some rookie might shoot them in a routine traffic stop. But tell the parents this softly, and offer a way out. That way out is you, the insurance investigator:

> Tell me where your boy is, Mrs. Doe. A fugitive's life is no way to live. I promise I won't hurt him and most importantly, Mrs. Doe, he will never know you told me. I promise you that.

And that is most important. *Never but never* burn your sources of information. You will be sued, screwed, and maybe shot.

Questions should emphasize solving the fugitive's problem. I will often say something like this to the party:

> All I'm trying to do is get this damn warrant off of Al's back. Remember, I'm not a cop. I'm with the appointment section at Acme Bonds and I'm trying to get him to sign a document to get the warrant taken care of.

Of course, the way you are going to help Al is by arresting him. But the language is soft and will in some cases open a door. Most of the people you speak to will resent having to lie for the fugitive and will look for a way to be helpful without being thought of as a stoolie or informant.

Here is where you must recognize the hesitant voice, the voice that disapproves of what the fugitive is doing, the voice of someone who is saying inside that they want to help, either because of some unknown revenge motive or out of true friendship with the fugitive.

Here, too, is where you might consider the possibility

of paying a reward or fee for information. This can be as little as $20 to as high as $1,000, or even more if necessary. The reward can be communicated over the phone to those who seem as though they want to be helpful yet need something in *exchange*, in the true meaning of the word. Dollars for information are well worth it and are a major weapon in a bounty hunter's arsenal.

If the case is serious enough financially, and you have a good relationship with the bail-bond agent, it is not unusual to split the informant's fee. Let's say you offer $500 for information on a $20,000 bail. You may be working for 10 percent or $2,000. A reward of $500 is a good chunk out of your fee. But what if your expenses are not that high and you could wrap this up in a week or ten days? Go for it. If the bondsman will split that with you, even better. But do it in either case. So what if you are "only" taking home $1,500. The fact of the matter is that you are probably putting out no more or less effort than you did when you only made $500 for finding a skip.

My point is that a $100,000 skip is no harder to find than a $5,000 skip. The basics still apply. Some of the bigger skips may have more money to flee the country, but it is a minor few that do. If the skip is like most other skips, he is still in the area and living a similar life-style as he did before he was arrested. So, a reward or fee for information should be accepted by you and can be used frequently. I know a lot of bounty hunters who won't utilize it for some reason, probably a false sense of pride. But it's just another weapon to get your man.

• • • • •

Phone soliciting for information will save you untold hours of labor and travel if the questions are thought out beforehand and are not arrogant in nature. Never use threats, as they will result in lawsuits against you or the bondsman at the least, and possibly criminal charges. You would be amazed at how many people tape their phone conversations.

Somewhere among all those numbers you have called is a friend. That friend will eventually evolve, maybe on the third call, maybe on the tenth, but he or she will surface. And either through trust, the reward, or revenge, that friend will tell you exactly where the fugitive is.

Just be patient.

CHAPTER SEVEN

Locating the Fugitive

Now the fun begins.

Concurrent with your phone inquiries with the fugitive's friends, enemies, relatives, and loved ones, you are doing some detective work, playing some tricks, and, in general, trying to find that rent money on the hoof.

You should start by checking the basic facets of the fugitive's life. These include, but are not limited to, his job (and, just as important, the type of work he does), car, interests, friends, and favorite foods.

Let's start with his job. Say our man is a stonemason. But he quit his job two days after skipping bail, probably because he saw a cop car drive by a job site or the business office and thought it was for him. So he bolted.

The reality is that the bench warrant the judge ordered has barely started trickling through the system, so the police don't even know that he is a fugitive yet. In fact, even after the warrant hits the local police department or sheriff's office, nothing much will happen. If the crime he was originally arrested for was particularly horrible, maybe a couple of detectives will check him out right away. Chances are they won't. With an average load of thirty to sixty cases, many detectives in medium-sized cities can't work the cases that quickly. It usually holds that the only person actively looking for the fugitive is the bounty hunter.

So by the time you get the order from the bondsman and gather the necessary paperwork, you check out his job and find he has left. He's also moved out of the trailer he lived in.

You don't think he has left the area, though, because his divorced wife lives nearby with their kid, whom he adores, and his own mom and dad are in the area. There is also a lot of building going on, therefore a good chance he will stay in the local trade. (Be he a stonemason, insurance agent, carpenter, or fisherman, most men will stay in the trade they know best. While this is not *always* true, it usually is.)

Logic dictates that you head right for the yellow pages and start a phone canvass of all the stonemason businesses listed there.

Make it simple; ask for the personnel department. In the smaller shops, a bookkeeper or even the owner will answer the phone. You can start your conversation something like this:

> Hello. This is Acme Department Store (use a large local chain) credit department calling. Mr. Doe has applied for credit and we want to verify his employment.

This is a simple statement that gets right to the gist of the matter. In all your inquiries but one you get a simple: "Gee, we have no Mr. Doe here." The whole conversation should take less than a minute. You simply thank the person and hang up, mumbling something about an incomplete application.

Calling all the stonemason businesses will take time and a possible increased phone bill if any are long distance. But it is cheaper than the gas and time it would take to drive to these places. Besides, phonework is at least

80 percent of bounty work, so you might as well get a lot of practice at it. If you cannot talk that easily over the phone, find an apprentice or girlfriend to do it for a cut of the pie. Women are generally better at it than men.

If you have no luck after a check of all the stone shops in the yellow pages, what do you do next? First, let's exhaust the stonemason theory before moving on. We know that the yellow pages closes out for advertising sometime in the fall. Would it hurt to check with the local business-licensing authority, city or county, to see if any stone shops have opened up *after* the yellow pages' advertising closed? Maybe he is working for one of these newer shops. Also, not everybody can afford to advertise in the yellow pages.

He, like any other tradesman, may be working out of a union hall, if his area has union labor. And don't overlook the possibility of him being an independent. On this you will have to check all the building sites in the area if his vehicle is parked nearby (you should know by now what kind of car he drives). You can also check with the general contractor to see if he has a subcontractor by the name of John Doe.

This kind of work is time consuming and laborious, but that's what you are getting paid for. Remember, you are not the type that can handle a 9-to-5 job.

At worst, your man is no longer in the stone trade. How do you find this out? Just ask questions about him at construction sites. And while you are at these sites, after you have asked if Doe or a subcontractor by that name was around, make the most of your time. Pass out a preprinted wanted poster (see Appendix D). I do this all the time and it takes little effort. A reward of $100 to $250 will attract a lot of interest. Include a phone number where you can be reached and expect calls all the time and at all hours. Generally, you will get your man.

This procedure can be followed for any interest the fugitive has. A lot of individuals in the building trades like to play pool. Usually there are no more than six to sixteen poolrooms in any medium-sized city or town. In the bigger cities you just have to allocate more time to look. Leave the wanted poster for your man with the owner, *always* stressing the confidentiality of any call made to you. I can't stress any more than you must honor that offering of confidence.

TRICKS OF THE TRADE

Often your man simply eludes all the logical steps you take to find him. You know he is in the area, as others have seen him or reported him to you.

There is the lottery gambit.

Most everyone has played the lottery. Chances are good your man has as well. Find the "state building" in your area. Various departments are run out of it, such as liquor enforcement and state taxes. Go in and look at the numbers on the doors and choose a nonexistent number. If the building has two stories, for example, pick a number such as 303.

Next, have a friend, preferably a woman, call one of the hotter phone numbers on your contact list (this call should be made on a Friday) and inform the answering party that:

> This is Mrs. Jones from the (state) Lottery Notification Commission. We have a winning ticket for Mr. Doe. Will he please come to our office at the state building, room 303, before 5:00 P.M. today?

Now, this ruse will only work if there is a system in your state lottery (should you even have one) where some tickets are winners in addition to the posted winning numbers. For instance, in California, some tickets have a symbol on them that allows one to participate in a spinning-wheel game, similar to roulette. The ticket is mailed into the capitol and individuals are notified by phone if they are a winner.

Should this be the case in your state, be prepared to stake out the state building for a half-day or day as the person you spoke to gets in touch with the fugitive. Chances are he will turn up there. Watch the parking lot and rear entrance if there is one. Expect to see some hopeful-looking person who appears very nervous as he is unable to find the right room number. This technique will uncover all but the more sophisticated skips.

Another trick of the trade is the money-order gambit. It costs $12 to send an amount of money via Western Union that is less than $50. Suppose you were to put into the system $5 addressed to your mark. With the $12 fee, that's a total outlay of $17.

Now have a woman friend call the subject's house and inform them that a money order from a book club, clearing house, or computer drawing has been won by Mr. Doe and for him to come to the nearest telegraph office to pick it up.

Generally, Western Union will not call to inform a recipient that a money order has arrived. A person must be looking for it and query them. Should the subject call Western Union to verify the money transfer, he will be told that, yes, there is some money awaiting him. The company will not disclose the amount over the phone, so this protects your small amount.

Most small towns and cities have three or four telegraph offices. When your friend calls, it is best to have her say: "This is the Main Street office and we are open until 6:00 P.M. (or whatever time). Can Mr. Doe come by as soon as possible so we don't have to send the money back? We have been trying to get him for several days and we are only allowed to keep it for seventy-two hours." Knowing full well that the fugitive has been running and inaccessible, the party on the line might pull out all stops to dig him up and get him down to the telegraph office.

Sometimes the telephoned party will want to know more about where the money came from. Your friend can coyly say, "Well, I shouldn't tell you this, but it is from a 'clearinghouse.' I can't tell you more." Everybody has heard of Ed McMahon and Publisher's Clearinghouse. That means money — big money.

Of course, this means a stakeout of the place in question, but that's the nature of this business. Bounty hunting is 95 percent boredom and 5 percent terror.

The lottery and money-order gambits are only two forms of pretexting that can be used to ferret out the bad guy or gal and/or information about them. There are other methods.

Posing as a fellow who was in jail with the fugitive, or even as the prison chaplain, has gained bounty hunters access to the fugitive via parents, loved ones, or buddies.

If your man has a motorcycle, especially a Harley-Davidson, you will either find him on it or see it parked at the Harley shop or where other Harley riders go. Unlike riders of Japanese bikes or other makes, Harley owners are a breed apart. They blend in to the social aspects of motorcycling easier than non-Harley riders. (Incidentally, I have had more skips who rode Japanese bikes than Harleys.)

Essentially, repeated questions to the same people, over and over, will find your man. Not demanding questions, unless you want a phone hung up on you, but sincere, deliberate, well-thought-out questions. If you find a person lying to you, give him his rope. Let him lie and eventually you will get to the truth. Mark Twain said, "Liars must have good memories." That sure is the truth. Eventually you will catch him lying and he will be embarrassed. At that point he will usually bend over backward to tell the truth.

You can also hint to less-aware contacts that they should not be harboring or in any way aiding or abetting a fugitive by lying for him. Let them know it's unwise to participate in the criminal events that John Doe is immersed in. Tell them that he has hurt a lot of innocent people, especially the collateral (who will have to pay the forfeit bail if you don't find the skip). Stress the bad this dude has done to his buddies. Have no qualms about lying, but make sure you do not jeopardize any innocent party, the bondsman, or yourself.

Placing a small ad in the classifieds for the specific skills your man may have will sometimes make him surface. Don't expect a result in five days though. Place the ad for thirty days (you can always cancel) and maybe you will get him in two. It works.

This is why it is good to have two telephone numbers. One you use for all bail-bond business and the other for false fronts like the one just mentioned. I may use my second number only five times a year. But I also use it for all outgoing calls to keep my legitimate business line clear. Hardly anyone knows my second number, not even my closest friends. That way I have no fear of answering, "Acme Trucking" or "State Lottery Commission" when it's part of the bait during an intense period of the pursuit.

One of the main things you did in the beginning was get a handle on the car your man drives. There are many services in this country that do nothing but supply motor vehicle data to insurance companies and private investigators. You can subscribe to one in your area, sometimes for as little as nothing down. Generally, you call them up and request an account number. This enables you to ask for an ownership check on a certain license plate, or if John Doe owns any cars in the Daytona Beach, Florida, area. If you don't know of any services, call around to some of the larger insurance agencies in your town, or check with some of the private investigators.

Usually these services charge from three to eight dollars per license check, and it's worth every dime. Your man may be driving a beat-up pickup truck while you are looking for a new Ford.

Remember, information is power. You can penetrate more areas and say a greater variety of things over the phone than any police officer can do. So be flexible and innovative. Create and enhance different approaches to ferret information out of those that hold it. And if all your glibness and intelligence won't do it, don't despair — there is always money.

CHAPTER EIGHT

Surveillance

No part of the bail-enforcement business is more tedious and tiresome than surveillance. Yet it must be done and done often. Most cases warrant a surveillance schedule; some only for a few hours, others for weeks. This work will be mind-boggling, eye-watering, and very, very wearing on you.

Surveillance can involve businesses, parents' homes, vehicles, and any number of other places. You will become just as suspicious to the neighborhood as the fugitive you are seeking, even to the point of having a police unit check on you.

This chapter will provide answers to these problems and outline the equipment you must have to carry out effective surveillance.

The need for surveillance can begin at anytime during the pursuit. In fact, once finding the address of any loved one or relative, one could make a case for surveilling that house immediately. Since you have nothing but time, this one and only case, and a burning desire to succeed, then do it!

A van with darkened windows on the sides and rear

Inside the author's van. When closed, the curtain effectively blackens the interior for surveillance. Note the shotgun rack, cellular phone, CB radio, police scanner, and storage cabinet. (Photo by John Taylor)

is perfect for surveillance. The rear windows should have curtains or blinds as well, and a thick, black curtain should be rigged up to run from roof to floor and side to side of the van just behind the front seats. This, when pulled across, will effectively seal off the rear section from any light coming in from the front. Since more than 60 percent of the streets in the United States run east to west, this will reduce the sunrise-sunset penetration of sun.

A darkened van is not only good for surveillance, it is also an excellent vehicle for the business of bail recovery itself. It allows one to keep all kinds of communication gear out of sight, provides private writing areas, and is perfect for the private transportation of prisoners. And, since the hours do get long in this business, a darkened van is excellent for pulling over to the side of the road or any all-night parking area to catch some needed sleep.

Given the address that you think the suspect is visiting, a decision to surveil must include the risks of discovery. Is the neighborhood "friendly" towards surveillance? For instance, a mixed neighborhood of light industrial and/or retail and residential buildings would be surveillance friendly. Plenty of traffic and strange cars would cover up your car's appearance as a new car in the area.

In setting up the surveillance, you must consider where the fugitive might park his car and the nearest door to the parking area. Assuming there are two entrances to a residence you are surveilling, which one would you choose to watch? Chances are the subject is not a professional fugitive, and his mind-set would allow him to enter as if he had no care in the world. Your vehicle should be parked close enough (within two blocks) to see the subject clearly yet avoid coming to the attention of the occupants of the surveilled residence. This is why binoculars are a must.

Any vehicle used in surveillance should be of a color and make that does not stand out in any neighborhood. If you are on a stakeout in a neighborhood of older Fords and Chevys, don't use your new BMW. Conversely, a neighborhood of BMWs and Mercedes Benzs should not be invaded by a run-down vehicle.

An ideal color for a stakeout van is either beige or white. A stakeout *passenger* vehicle, however, should not be either of these colors. Many passenger cars used by authorities just happen to be in beige or white. Faded blue or green might be better. Some oddball bumper stickers would help draw attention away from the possibility of it being an "official" car, too.

As I mentioned earlier, van windows should be very dark, with curtains or cardboard held in place over the window *behind* the one you are looking out to preclude being silhouetted by the light behind you. If your windows have metal frames, hardware store magnets glued onto the corners of cardboard (cut to size and painted flat black) work just fine.

On a longer stakeout of, let's say twenty-four hours a day for three to five days, someone else should drive the van to the selected spot, especially if your insertion is during the day. Then have the driver get out and leave in a second vehicle driven by an assistant. This leaves you and a buddy in the sealed-off back of the van for surveillance. This procedure is not so necessary if your setup is done in the early hours of the morning, although there is always a chance of *someone* being awake who just happens to be looking out a window as your van pulls up.

Should you need to get out of the van at night, it is imperative that opening the door does not activate the interior light. This can be avoided by simply duct-taping a Popsicle stick over the plunger in the doorframe that activates the light. This will keep the plunger down, and the stick prevents it from wearing through the tape.

Another point about getting out of any surveillance vehicle at night: don't fret about closing the door all the way. This is hard to do without drawing attention, even with a modest slam. Just close the door until you hear a click.

In addition to your wits, you will need something for a urinal (such as a Porta-Potty), lots of fruit or munchies, and a circulating fan on the roof. The best fans for this can be found not at van- or auto-supply stores, but at yachting stores. Little fans that are placed on cabin ceilings and run by wind only are very quiet and efficient. You should also have a police scanner, a small radio, and a fold-out, multicushion lounge chair. One party can snooze while the other watches. A good system is a two-hour watch at night and a longer watch during the day.

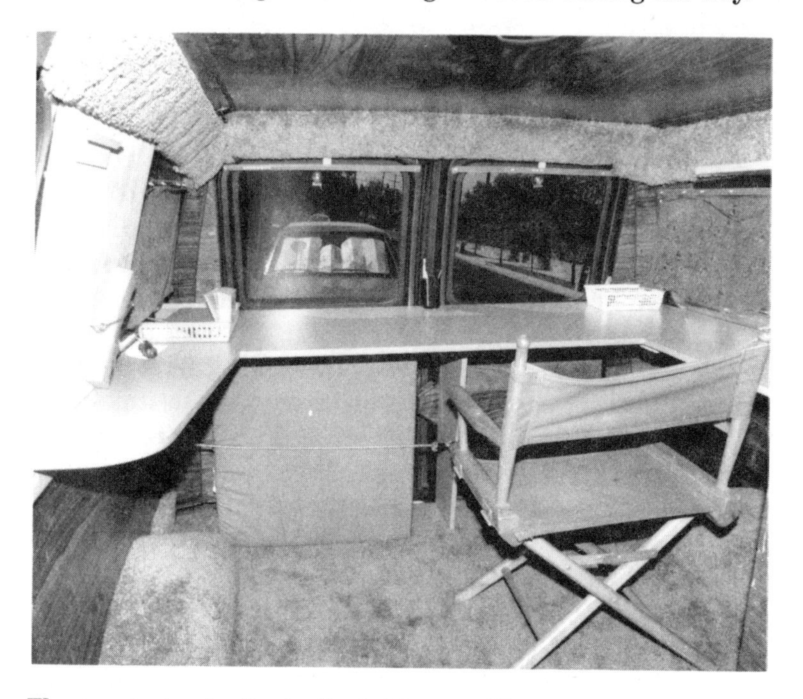

The countertop in the back of this surveillance van can be used for taking notes and writing reports as well as allowing for more comfortable seating during long hours of surveillance. (Photo by John Taylor)

Should you be in a passenger car, the surveillance will be more obvious. A San Francisco cop once told me that there are only two reasons for two men to stay in a car after it parks: either they are gays or they are detectives. Remember, it is "normal" for a person or two to pull to the curb, load or unload their car, and walk or drive away. It is not normal for them to sit there for hours on end.

When using a private passenger car, there are several tricks of the trade to minimize the surveillance or narc role you might project. Try to arrive on the scene around dawn so not too many people see you pull up. On arriving, get out and fuss around in the trunk, then reenter the car and sit on the *passenger side* for the balance of the day. This looks like you are waiting for your "buddy." And bring some newspapers and other reading material; it makes you look less businesslike.

Consider going to a store that makes magnetic signs and getting one or two made that say "Acme Traffic Surveys." Place them on the side of the car. When arriving on the site, bring out your canvas director's chair with the little umbrella attached, a clipboard, and orange vest à la the road construction crews. Sit out there all day ostensibly counting cars but really watching and waiting. This works and takes the nervousness out of the stakeout. It would not hurt to have a chart with hour-by-hour segments of vehicle traffic counts in case a neighborhood busybee comes over and chats with you. You are a contract agent with Acme and the county is considering a stop sign, a stoplight, or widening the street. Simple pretexting.

These magnetic signs can be made in any format. It wouldn't hurt to inquire if there are any signs not picked up after being ordered and made. You might get a good buy on some unwanted signs. One bounty hunter in California has a plumber's sign on his van. Piled on the overhead rack are a couple dozen pipes, fitting the picture very well.

To preclude a visit from the police should an active

member of Neighborhood Watch find you and your stakeout suspicious, it is important to visit the watch commander of the local police department, or precinct if it's a big city. The card in Appendix D should be used (or something like it) to let the officer know that you will be on a surveillance in a certain neighborhood. He'll then inform his dispatcher and the officers of various shifts of your presence so they won't bother you should a call come in reporting a suspicious parked vehicle.

It is very disruptive to be interrupted in the middle of a surveillance by an officer wanting to know what you are doing in the neighborhood. You will need to check into the station each day to make sure the new officer coming on duty is aware of your presence.

This is why a good police scanner is a must. It is very easy to program in all the police frequencies in your area of operation. In addition to listening to them for enjoyment, it might also prove life-saving should a maniac be running toward your neck of the woods and you are exposed to view.

More importantly, a police scanner will enable you to hear a dispatcher requesting a patrol unit to check you out. That's right; *your* car is being described on the air because some neighbor called in a suspicious vehicle. In order to avoid blowing your surveillance, leave the scene immediately, go to a well-lit restaurant, and call the police dispatcher right away. Inform him that you are the driver of the vehicle in question and it is a bail-bond matter. Tell him you are at the restaurant and are willing to meet the patrol unit. Describe yourself (e.g., white male, dark hair, blue jacket, age 39). Stand under a bright light and, if it is not a Friday or Saturday night, you will probably meet the patrol officer within thirty minutes. More than likely he will completely understand what's going on, maybe over coffee. Do it right and you will be back on site within an hour. This is just part of the business and it is to be expected.

Surveillance has become much easier in the past few years thanks to the addition of one tool of modern civilization: the cellular car phone. One of my minor claims to fame is that I was the first bounty hunter in history to use this device. Now they are quite common; in fact, one very efficient bounty hunter, Lance Wilkinson of New Hampshire, has two in his car. He has used them in most of his cases over the past two years. They save time, energy, gas, and money.

Many times the scenario for cellular-phone usage would go like this. The neighborhood does not appear to be surveillance friendly, and it is important that you not be seen there. That being the case, I approach some of the neighbors that I found in earlier discussions to be friendly and potentially helpful and offer them a $100 bill (or $20 or $50, depending on the value of the contract) if they call me at this number as soon as the bad guy arrives. Now if I lived ten minutes away I would use my home phone, but I'm more like an hour away. The neighbor now has my cellular car-phone number. I head right for a friendly restaurant or saloon, bring in my transportable phone (the kind that comes out of the car with its own battery power pack is best for this business) and some papers, and start reading, sipping, and/or eating.

It rarely fails; I will receive a call from a breathless voice saying, "He's here," and back I go to arrest the just-burned fugitive.

Before I leave you with the wrong impression, while I am sitting in that saloon waiting for the call, *I never drink alcohol*. Period! No one should while working a case.

The cellular phone can also be used when you have only one person in the van on surveillance. That person, on sighting the fugitive, can call his working partner or the police for a backup.

What if the fugitive comes out before anyone arrives to help with the arrest? This is a decision you must make based on your size, the size of the fugitive, his history of violence, his crime, and the proximity of his friends. I have found it comfortable to make many arrests depending on just myself and my displayed but holstered revolver.

If the subject should leave by car and no help has arrived and you are not inclined to arrest him by yourself, there is a simple way to proceed. Follow at a prudent distance and call the police dispatcher. Inform the dispatcher that you are following a car driven by a felony fugitive who is in the system (more on this later) and request a police backup. State that you were at such and such address originally and had to follow the fugitive and are now proceeding up I-95 toward Cocoa Beach, for example. Within minutes, you will have police all around and your subject will be in custody.

Where you will have difficulty is if the subject is the perpetrator of a misdemeanor or if he is a collateral-withdrawal arrest. The police won't get involved in the latter (other than a drive-by to "keep the peace") and won't always rush on a misdemeanor.

There are several books on the subject of surveillance and they are worth having in your library. I did not discuss tailing or following a subject in detail, as this rarely comes about. Besides, if you see your subject, you won't be tailing him — you'll be arresting him.

CHAPTER NINE

The Arrest

The arrest is the culmination and satisfaction of a job done and, hopefully, done well. You are coming face-to-face with an individual whom you have lived with, in name and personality only, for a few weeks or months. He might have known you were tracking him and perhaps you even walked by him once without knowing it. But now the moment of truth is upon you.

You are going to be depriving an individual of his or her freedom. This event can generate the most violent reaction in some fugitives and a shrug of the shoulders in others. No two individuals will react the same way. Yet they can be divided into two groups: those who resist and those who don't.

Statistically, the odds are greatly in your favor that the subject will come along peacefully. In my own experience I have found that less than 3 percent will resist violently. But that is not the only type of resistance. Another small percentage will try to run as you are searching them or right before you put on the handcuffs. Yet most will come along in a very passive manner, making the job at hand worthwhile.

But remember, any arrest, even for the most insignificant infraction, should be regarded as a potentially dangerous situation. We will discuss here a situation that does not involve any shooting. That rare and horrible event of being required to shoot someone is best left for another book. Here we will address taking someone into custody in a safe and harmless fashion, how to handcuff and search them, and their journey back to jail.

An arrest could occur in a fast-food store, the subject's home, a friend's residence, a gas station (under surveillance as a frequented site), on the street, or anywhere else you can imagine. It might not even be planned. You may be sitting at a traffic light and see your target walking across the street in front of you. Ideally, your detective work will lead you to a residence that an informant indicated was a likely spot for the subject to frequent. Maybe his girlfriend lives there or he does dope there.

In practice, the arrest at a residence is the most common. Arrest at a business or workplace would have to be a close second, at least in my experience.

ARMED AND DANGEROUS

Despite my statement that very few skips resist arrest, you must assume, at the moment of a face-to-face encounter, that your fugitive is armed and potentially dangerous. Assume he has a weapon or something he could use as a weapon on his person (for example, never overlook a woman's high heels) or hidden somewhere within reach. Keep an eye on his friends nearby, too.

It is imperative to assume total control of the fugitive on first contact This can be done verbally, with a weapon you have displayed, or by physical control or perhaps physical force.

A typical encounter begins this way:

You: "Mr. Doe, you are under arrest for failure to appear."

Fugitive: "¢&$#*! I went to court! Everything is in order!"

Two bounty hunters search an arrested fugitive. The hunter on the right, Bob Burton, just became aware of the approaching wife of the subject. She had to be restrained. (Photo by Dave Brucker)

You: "Not so. The police have a warrant for you (don't say this if not true) and the bondsman has authorized your arrest. Turn around and place your hands on the wall (or turn around, kneel on the floor, and place your hands behind your back)."

Usually he will comply while still protesting. If he is slow, you will have to exert some guiding pressure. While talking to the subject, grasp his arm and steer him into a controllable position. I am well over six feet and weigh 230 pounds, so my presence alone often aids in subduing the fugitive.

Others of more moderate size would be advised to have an assistant of substantial size and intellect — one who is *not* prone to violence or has an uncontrollable temper. Actually, all hunters should always have a backup with

Hamp George, Hawaiian bounty hunter, and author Bob Burton.

them. I usually pick my backup based on speed. Due to my size, I'm not much of a sprinter. I'm fine across a living room or down several flights of stairs, but all-out sprinting across rooftops . . . well, that's better left to a younger and faster person. So, I'm sort of the pit bull and my partner is the Doberman.

Perhaps your best ally is surprise. Never allow your fugitive to mentally or physically prepare for your arrival. It does no good to call him up and tell him you are coming over the get him. Should you happen to someday find your man this way, resist that impulse.

After your twentieth or thirtieth arrest, some of the nervousness will fade. Until then, however, you will find yourself out of breath when arresting a skip. Your nervousness will cause you to forget items (like handcuffs) and, in general, generate an overall uncomfortable feeling, which is all quite natural. You are a civilian, after all, and you are not doing this eight hours a day. The advantage you have is unstructured guidelines, maybe some creativity, and the ability to say and do things that police officers are forbidden to do.

A true national bounty hunter who is tops in the Northeast is Lance Wilkinson. He has some thoughts on arrest that are worth passing on here:

> In every arrest situation, the agent must be firm and prepared to protect himself. Force, which will vary from verbal to actual physical contact, is vital to *control* the fugitive. A fugitive who is peacefully submitting must not be manhandled or physically abused. Resistance, on the other hand, should be met with sufficient force to overcome the subject's resistance and no more. The key operative word is *reasonable*. Anything more than reasonable could involve you and the bonds agent in a civil lawsuit.

DEADLY FORCE

Firearms and the potential of having to use them are part and parcel of being a bail enforcement agent. Yet the use of deadly force is a serious matter. Justification of deadly force is only possible in the defense of human life, and then only as a last resort.

Brandishing a firearm is never advised in the course of an arrest unless you feel your life may be in danger. This should be more manifest than simple nervousness or edginess. The subject must have a reputation for violence with weapons, have been convicted of a violent crime, or promised not to be "taken alive." The arrest of a subject for jumping bail on a drunk-driving charge would not be a good time for a lot of gun waving. This is not to say that you should not carry a firearm, just don't develop the mentality that you can't arrest or work without it.

In approximately 60 percent of the cases I bring to jail, I do not carry a firearm. After a while you will develop a sense for which situations warrant a firearm carry.

So-called "warning shots" are neither warranted nor justified. You could easily wind up in the same cell as the person you came to arrest. Shooting a fleeing fugitive cannot be done unless that fugitive is both fleeing and turning around taking potshots at you. If he is a well-known rapist or major threat to the comunity, then public mores may well condone your shooting him in the back, but don't count on it.

THE FRISK

So you have a subject standing against a wall, hands spread apart, and you and your partner are searching him. A cursory search for weapons large enough to be detected easily is called a "frisk" or "pat down."

A "field search" is a more detailed and laborious method. This entails grasping and squeezing every part of clothing on the fugitive. This includes pockets, crotch area, trouser legs, underarms, and so on. I will often turn up marijuana or cocaine during these searches. I simply give the stuff a heave-ho with an admonishment to the fugitive that he doesn't need any more problems than he already has. He knows the jailers will frisk him and he is usually grateful that you took the drugs out of his pants. My suggestion is not to keep it or put it on your person in any way, but to throw it away then and there. It is illegal contraband and you don't need the hassle either.

Seldom do I find a weapon on prisoners, except for things that could be used for legitimate purposes such as pocket knives and nail files, but nothing more serious. Should the fugitive have a hidden weapon that you miss in a frisk and you bring him to jail with the weapon on him, you will face ridicule and a loss of trust (in addition to endangering your own life). Remember, when you get to the jail the correctional officers will search your man thoroughly. They will expect you to have done a good job

Marshall Rowles frisking a fugitive while Bob Burton looks on.

of searching him before bringing him in. You had best do so. You do not need a reputation as one who sloppily brings in armed prisoners.

Don't let any inhibitions stop you from searching a woman prisoner. Search her purse and remove high heels if she is wearing them. Look for hat pins and hairpins as well. When making a female arrest, I always have a female backup along to do a more thorough body search.

If you are by yourself, I advise having the prisoner lie prone on the floor. Have him place his hands behind his back. Then handcuff and search him while he remains in that position. Generally, your success in searching will be the same as if he were standing, with less risk of flight or fight.

Should the fugitive be violence-prone and/or facing a

stiff sentence, be ready for trouble. During these situations it is best to have your fellow agent either cover the subject with a firearm or hold onto the man's shoulder while you frisk. Any move the fugitive makes will be first transmitted from the shoulder, and your assistant will feel it and be instantly prepared for what is coming.

Most problems can be eliminated by handcuffing the skip before searching. Remember, you are arresting him regardless of what he says or what is in his pockets. The determination to arrest or rearrest was made the day you got the contract from the bonds agent.

HANDCUFFS

Placing handcuffs on an individual requires correct placement in order to avoid trouble. Always place the handcuffs on the fugitive's wrists with his hands *behind* his back. With your prisoner in a controllable position (kneeling, prone, or against the wall) have him bring his right arm back first, with the palm facing outward. Secure the cuff on this wrist and then have him bring his left arm back in the same fashion and secure the other wrist. Some agents slip the cuffs under the subject's belt before cuffing the final wrist to further secure him. This will prevent a more agile person from stooping down and slipping his feet through the cuffed wrists to bring his arms up in front of him.

Occasionally you may find someone who, because of a physical deformity, will require the cuffs to be in front. This can be accomplished by taking his belt off, slipping it over the interconnecting links of the cuffs, and rebuckling the belt behind him. A more professional way is to use police-style waist restraints that can be bought at police supply stores. For more violent types, or those who you think might try to run, leg shackles are available as well. These are also good for long intrastate or interstate trips.

Any bail enforcement agent should have at least two

Discussing the bail bond problem with a bail fugitive.

good pairs of handcuffs. Peerless and Smith & Wesson are two of the better brands.

Once in a while you will have custody of two bail skips. The search patterns are the same; but if you only have one set of handcuffs, there is a safe way to cuff two people. Handcuff the right wrist of one to the right wrist of the other, backs to each other. With some planning, though, you will have brought along at least two sets of cuffs to avoid this problem.

CHAPTER TEN

On Weapons

Minimize the use of a gun as much as possible. Most bounty hunters have gotten into trouble with their *own* gun rather than any bad guy's gun. Trouble comes from the stupid waving and brandishing of a firearm in a public place as well as its actual use.

Most arrests can be effected without the use of a firearm since most defendants are jumping bail on nonviolent crimes and will not resist arrest. I carry a firearm in about 40 percent of my arrests; I carry it in the vehicle 50 percent of the time in case I should need it.

Generally, by the time you are in a position to arrest the fugitive, you have gotten a picture of him or her that will determine your need to carry a weapon or not. My criteria for bringing a weapon are:

1. He has jumped on a serious assault charge.
2. He is gang connected.
3. He is from a large family who might resist or turn on me.
4. I suspect he lives in a crack house or similar dwelling.
5. The suspect is known to resist arrest.

Another reason to bring a gun is simply the intuition that says "be careful." Sometimes you don't know why, but a sixth sense tell you to watch out.

If the fugitive does resist, in most cases he will do so physically. This will entail trying to run away, fight, or simply resist your attempt to handcuff him. This last scenario could be nothing more than a lot of wiggling, trying to keep you from snagging his wrists for cuffing. Pulling out a pistol and threatening him would be a most foolish thing to do.

A pistol should never be brandished or pointed unless you are prepared to shoot that person and can later justify the shooting. Just because you are making a lawful arrest does not mean you are allowed to carry a gun, much less shoot someone. In one jurisdiction in Texas, a district attorney said that any bondsman using force to subdue a fugitive would be prosecuted. And he wasn't even talking about a firearm.

Often nothing more dangerous than a flashlight is necessary for an arrest.

One of the common problems facing a bounty hunter is entering a house with a pistol or shotgun in plain view when the subject is not there. Despite having probable and justifiable cause for entering the house, you will probably be arrested and charged with a Breaking and Entering or Burglary complaint by the owners, or whoever was there during your entry. The charge will be made worse by the waving of a gun. This happens every year to some bounty hunter. Of course there are hundreds, probably thousands of forcible entries made by recovery agents that go unnoticed or unchallenged, especially when the fugitive is caught.

In many states a concealed-weapons permit is easily obtainable. This would be fine for the working recovery agent that feels the need for a weapon and a need to conceal. Other states, where it is more difficult to obtain a permit (or impossible), will still allow any citizen to carry a weapon while making a lawful arrest. This is a common-law right in most states. Part of your research is to find the areas that allow you to carry a weapon. After all, the reality of this business is that there will be some situations in which you will need a weapon.

I have been talking about handguns as concealable weapons. Ironically, the laws are more lax toward non-concealable weapons, such as rifles or shotguns. A short-stocked shotgun is as portable as a pistol and is far more deadly. Its very presence is intimidating to whomever sees it. Everybody respects a shotgun. It isn't considered a concealable weapon, and the laws are less restrictive in its use, or at least the carrying of it.

In researching your right to carry a weapon while making an arrest, resist asking the police about it. They have a tendency to discourage and mislead a citizen in this area. I think they have a basic idea that the fewer armed citizens, the safer the police are. I can't fault them on that, but do your own research. Check the penal or criminal codes on citizen's arrests, concealed weapons, and so on. Of course, your local bondsman will know about this subject, as will the local recovery agent.

I will often carry my weapon under an untucked shirt, such as a Hawaiian-style shirt. It is concealed and readily available. It allows me to get close to the bad guy without him seeing the weapon and going on full alert. If the police turn up, I can easily tuck the shirt into my waist, allowing for the pistol to be "open carry," a form allowed in most (but not all) states while making a lawful arrest.

Part of the trouble a novice recovery agent has is getting the mystique of the "bounty hunter" out of his mind. Despite books, television, and movies, one cannot put a weapon to a fugitive's head sitting in a crowded McDonald's on a Saturday afternoon and not expect some trouble from the cops for brandishing a weapon. If the fugitive is a mass-murder suspect as well as a rapist, you will probably get away with any overreaction. But if it's a run-of-the-mill drunk driver, dope user, petty thief, or hit-and-run driver, you simply can't pull a gun unless he is armed.

If you are concerned about subduing the fugitive, bring along one of your larger and more physical friends. Even then, use common sense, as you must take the prisoner alive. Don't pick a friend who might be a bit overreactive or prone to violence. You, your friend, and the bondsman that hired you will end up in a lawsuit if you use anything but *reasonable force*. Reasonable is the operative word here for everything.

I have a file of horror stories about bounty hunters being arrested for waving weapons where they shouldn't be doing so. Besides questioning their professional common sense, I also wonder about the bondsmen who hired them in the first place. Did the bondsman even know how many oars this "bounty hunter" had in the water? Had he worked with the hunter before? Were there any telltale signs of instability or lack of common sense? Many times, an arrest of a bounty hunter stems from the fact that he wasn't a recovery agent in the first place, just someone hunting bounty. Maybe he had never taken anyone into custody before, or had three or four belts of whiskey before going to make the arrest. A deadly combination: a weak mind, whiskey, and a weapon.

I won't be so arrogant as to second-guess the area you work in and your personal need for a weapon. My basic philosophy is that it is better to be tried by twelve good men than carried by six. But you must seriously consider the need for a weapon in any given situation. Don't carry it just because of the trade. Be aware that you can be arrested as easily as the fugitive you seek if you violate any weapons laws. And even if you beat the rap, you won't miss the ride downtown. It can ruin your whole day.

CHAPTER ELEVEN

"Is he in the system?"

"The system." You will hear that phrase often in this business. If the fugitive is in the system, it will be a major help in making an arrest in locations unfamiliar to you, and it will help document your authority.

The "system" refers to a data bank maintained by the Federal Bureau of Investigation (FBI) and called the National Crime Information Center, universally referred to as NCIC.

A nationwide, user-oriented information system, NCIC supports almost 60,000 police officers, sheriffs, highway patrolmen, coastal patrols, and, in general, all law-enforcement and criminal-justice agencies in the United States on a twenty-four-hour basis. The Royal Canadian Mounted Police (RCMP) and police agencies in Puerto Rico and the Virgin Islands access the system as well.

In addition to housing bulletins on criminals, criminal records, warrants outstanding, and wanted individuals, NCIC also is a central index for foreign fugitives, unidentified and missing persons, persons posing a threat to U.S. Secret Service protectees (the president, visiting VIPs, etc.), stolen property (such as boats, guns, securities, and license plates), and Originating Agency Identifiers, which identifies the agency that entered the record.

Within the juvenile category of the NCIC Missing Person File is the Missing Children File. It utilizes a unique method of entry, as it allows the parent, legal guardian, or next-of-kin to enter the system. As it happens, many local police departments will not immediately enter a missing child into the system after a request to do so by the parents. The reason for this is that many localities and states have restricting rules and regulations for using the system. Also, the police might feel that the child is not missing in a criminal fashion but may have run away for a while, with eventual return in the cards. Yet the system allows the distraught parents to go to the nearest FBI office and an effort will be made to ensure immediate entry. This is FBI policy.

In July of 1987, the Foreign Fugitive File was implemented into NCIC. This file contains wanted-persons records for foreign nationals entered by the United States National Central Bureau of the Interpolice Organization (INTERPOL).

NCIC handles almost one million requests a day. These range from an officer checking a suspicious driver on a routine traffic stop to a booking of an armed robbery suspect. In 1988, 132,000 wanted persons were apprehended using the system. You will be using the system as well.

TRIPLE I

The Interstate Identification Index, called "Triple I," is an improved concept for the interstate exchange of criminal history records. Triple I provides the criminal justice community with access to more than twelve million individual criminal history records maintained by the FBI's Identification Division and twenty participating criminal history data bases. The FBI Identification Division is sort of like the fifty-first state. It holds federal criminal history records and temporarily serves as a surrogate for nonparticipating states of Triple I.

When NCIC receives an on-line request for a criminal history record maintained in one of the participating states, NCIC automatically sends a message to the state computer, which will provide the record directly to the requesting agency. All records are supported by a fingerprint card completed at the time of arrest.

The twenty participating states providing on-line criminal history information as of this writing are: California, Colorado, Connecticut, Delaware, Florida, Georgia, Idaho, Michigan, Minnesota, Missouri, New Jersey, New York, North Carolina, Ohio, Oregon, Pennsylvania, South Carolina, Texas, Virginia, and Wyoming.

NCIC 2000

NCIC 2000 is an attempt by the FBI to meet the changing needs of the law-enforcement community for the interstate exchange of documented criminal justice data. The 2000 system is in the planning and development stage as of this writing, but this much is known: heavy emphasis will be placed on artificial intelligence and image transmission. (Artificial intelligence is the ability of a machine to think, reason, or learn. It is the ultimate goal of computer science.) Searching techniques and overall performance will be improved.

All this translates into a patrol unit being able to have a fax-like machine in the car that will receive a photograph of the subject just stopped for running a light, in addition to any current wanted data. Also, a tube-like device in the patrol car, into which the subject places his finger, will provide complete verification of the individual's ID and criminal records.

STATE SYSTEMS

NCIC is a federal system and not every felon winds up in it. Often something breaks down, or a later felony charge is filed way after an initial misdemeanor arrest, and NCIC is not notified. Therefore, you must be aware of your own state's system.

Your state system will be in use locally, and the identifying number for your case can be one of many systems. Often, the case number is used as the warrant number. The case number can be found (usually) on the letter of forfeiture the bondsman receives from court informing him that the subject is now a Failure To Appear.

If you don't know your warrant number, simply call the local police or sheriff's office and ask for "Warrants" or "Fugitive Detail." Identify yourself and explain what you are doing. You will need the subject's date of birth and possibly his Social Security number. Most times the officer will be more than helpful. Sometimes, however, you will run into a stonehead. If this happens, see who you know in the community who knows an officer who can obtain the information for you. It even works sometimes to simply approach a patrol unit and have them run it over the car radio.

Having these numbers is most important in bail enforcement. It ensures police participation at the time of the arrest, especially with felonies. For instance, it is not uncommon to make a surprise arrest of your subject, such as when you run across him unexpectedly in a restaurant or at a gas station. It happens all the time. Having the warrant numbers with you in a situation such as this will expedite the police response. If you call the police or sheriff for a backup (assuming you have time), it will not be forthcoming unless you can give the dispatcher or watch commander some numbers to indicate that this is truly a "wanted" man.

With a warrant number, the police are obliged to respond in a timely fashion, especially if it is a felony. If you are by yourself and reluctant to make the arrest, this is the best way to handle it. If, however, you have a working friend with you and/or if you think there is little chance of your fugitive resisting, make the arrest yourself. But don't start waving a gun so someone calls the police and has you arrested along with the bad guy!

In any case, bail enforcement work is a matter of numbers. Those numbers are extremely important to the system that you must work within. It is important for you to realize this in order to get your job done efficiently, keep the police happy and develop a good rapport with them, and get the exoneration you had promised the bondsman in order to secure the arrest contract in the first place.

CHAPTER TWELVE

On Contracts

I am often asked if I have written contracts with bail-bond agents. My answer is that in thirty years of experience in bail enforcement, the last eleven years being the most intensive, I have never had a written contract. I have only been burned once, and that, ironically, was by another bounty hunter. He had come to California from Florida and requested my assistance in a case one afternoon in 1986. Using my car, I assisted him in picking up a ranch worker who had jumped out of West Palm Beach. I even did most of the finding. He gave me a "check's in the mail" bit as he left town and that was the last I saw of him. Despite repeated calls, I just got lots of BS in return and not one dime. Alas, payback is a bitch.

Perhaps the one time you will use a contract is when the collateral wants to get off the loan as the cosigner. In this case, you are working for that person under the cover of a revoked bail.

I have used the contract in Appendix D with cosigners on several occasions. Perhaps you, too, will find it comfortable to use. Have it signed in front of a witness, and don't be afraid to ask for some start-up money. A retainer of $200 to $500 would not be out of line. It depends on how much travel you will have to do, the amount of the bail, how dangerous the suspect, and how well-heeled the customer.

CHAPTER THIRTEEN

Your Arrest (and How to Avoid It)

One of the hazards of this job is getting arrested yourself. Yes, that's true. You are hooked up, searched, and booked. Arrested. How could that happen? You have the same interests as the police: find and arrest bad guys. Don't they know you're on their side?

Well, the facts of life are that most bounty hunters wind up getting arrested or, at the very least, detained at least once in their career. If one is truly a full-time bounty hunter, it could easily happen two or three times. No one is immune.

One of our members, a bondsman/bounty hunter for his own agency and others, a retired deputy sheriff, and a former Navy SEAL, got thrown into jail recently when he went into a house in Oklahoma to find a fugitive. He entered the house only after waiting for at least five hours for police backup, including making a request in person to some officers having coffee. He spent two days in jail before being bailed out. Eventually charges were dropped, and now he is suing the city, county, and the officers.

Although the fugitive wasn't in the house — or, more likely, was hiding within the house — the officers arrived while our man was searching. Their timing was unbelievable, even more so when it turned out that one of the patrolmen was related to the owner of the house. You get it—a setup.

In every jurisdiction in the United States there is at least one officer who would like to bust a bounty hunter. For what reason? It could be resentment of our authority to arrest, or knowing a hunter that beat the cop to an arrest. It could be anything. Your job is to walk the line of common sense during all bail enforcement operations.

Notify the police when operating in their area (if you find it feasible). Also, refrain from entering a house in a strange town, county, or state unless you have documented all the facts, especially the probability of the fugitive being in the house.

Try to make an arrest without too many witnesses. They will call the police if they don't know what's happening and you could be arrested or at least detained.

Don't dress like a homeless person. Your clothing and demeanor will have a great effect on the way the police react to you.

Avoid the open display of firearms of any kind. This will do nothing but agitate the situation. The newspaper clippings indicate some of the problems you can run into.

Excessive force is not allowed in this business. When it happens, you immediately become a kidnapper, thug, or worse, a felon. You could, in fact, wind up in the same cell as the fugitive you arrested.

The areas that get bounty hunters in trouble, especially in urban areas where you will be noticed easily, are:

1. Open display and brandishing of firearms.
2. Entering a house recklessly—crashing through doors or windows, pushing the occupants around, pretending to be a police officer, etc.
3. Excessive force in dealing with a fugitive.

Being a bail enforcement agent gives you a great deal

GRABBED BY BOUNTY HUNTERS

Canadian freed from jail 2 years after abduction

TORONTO (AP) — Two years after Sidney L. Jaffe was grabbed by bounty hunters while jogging, hustled across the U.S. border and jailed in Florida, the Canadian businessman who became entangled in a diplomatic dispute is home and free.

Jaffe arrived Tuesday night at the Toronto airport about six hours after a judge's order permitted him to walk out the door at Florida's Avon Park Correctional Institution. He had been serving time for failure to appear in court in connection with charges of unlawful land sales.

Jaffe, 58, a native of New York and a naturalized Canadian citizen, hugged his wife and daughter and told reporters he would celebrate.

"Now's the time we're going to open the case of wine we bought in France," he said. "I'm not going to drink it all tonight, but I'm going to get a good start on it."

The ordeal began when Jaffe failed to appear in court on charges of unlawful land sales practices, and bounty hunters brought him to Florida. Prosecutors there said hundreds of investors lost more than $2 million in the 1970s in a development called St. Johns Riverside Estates in Putnam County.

Jaffe blames Nortek Inc., the company that sold him the land, and has filed suit in federal court in Miami against Nortek.

Canadian officials were infuriated by the affair, calling it a breach of sovereignty and a violation of its extradition treaty with the United States. Diplomatic pressure was applied at top levels and the affair was described as a serious strain on relations.

Eventually Secretary of State George P. Shultz appealed to Florida to let Jaffe go and Canada filed suit against the state to try to win his freedom.

Jaffe's conviction on 28 counts of unlawful land sales practices were overturned in September by a state appeals court, which left standing a conviction and five-year sentence for failing to appear to stand trial.

Last week the Florida Parole and Probation Commission approved Jaffe's release on the basis of his 19 months served at the medium-security prison, but ordered him into the custody of Putnam County officials because bond had not been posted on a remaining charge of organized fraud.

On Tuesday, Circuit Judge Edwin Sanders in Avon Park approved a $150,000 bond arrangement backed by a letter of credit from a Tallahassee bank to permit Jaffe's release.

Jaffe's attorneys are fighting to dismiss the remaining fraud charge, but the businessman said he would return willingly to Florida to face the charge if necessary.

When the trial date came up in April 1981 on the illegal land practices charges, Jaffe remained in Toronto, saying he had injured his head during a pickup basketball game and could not travel for medical reasons.

Arizona jury won't indict bounty hunters

A father-and-son team of California bounty hunters arrested on charges of first-degree murder last month has been freed after a grand jury refused to indict them, authorities said.

According to law-enforcement officials and attorneys familiar with the case, Arizona law and federal-court rulings give bounty hunters "a license to kill" when pursuing bail jumpers in Arizona.

The incident involves the death of Richard Monroe Bachellor, 24, of Riverside, who was fatally shot in the back in a parking lot in north Phoenix.

2 bounty hunters arrested

By Bruce Finley
Denver Post Staff Writer

AURORA — Two self-described bounty hunters accused of beating a fugitive truck driver before delivering him to Adams County Jail early Saturday have been jailed themselves.

Larry Hamilton, 30, and Joseph Wilkens, 40, are accused of using a 2-by-4 and tire iron to hit Denver truck driver Larry Johnson, 29, breaking his ribs and knuckles.

They went "way too far," said Aurora Police Detective Frank White. "That's not the way to handle it."

Johnson had failed to appear in Adams County Court on charges of possession of cocaine.

He was wanted for violating a $20,000 bond, as well as breaking Texas parole conditions imposed after he served a jail sentence for indecency to children.

Late Friday, the bounty hunters broke into the Aurora home of Johnson's girlfriend and forced her at gunpoint to lead them to Johnson at a Xenia Street apartment in Denver, detectives said.

Witnesses gave conflicting accounts on whether gunshots were fired.

"There's no doubt that they held him (Johnson) back and assaulted him," White said.

The bounty hunters arrived at the jail with Johnson about 1:30 a.m., jail officials said.

Detectives said they suspect other men may have been involved in the hunt for Johnson.

"There's more to it than meets the eye," said White, who did not know who, if anyone, had hired Hamilton and Wilkens to track Johnson.

Hamilton was released on $60,000 bond, but Wilkens remained in jail. Both face felony kidnapping and burglary charges.

Johnson received medical treatment before being booked into the jail.

Two other bounty hunters were arrested a week ago in Grand Junction after they kicked down the door of an apartment in Denver and dragged away the pajamas-clad resident.

Although a 40-year-old U.S. Supreme Court ruling gives bounty hunters for bail bondsmen extraordinary police powers, Denver's district attorney said such powers do not extend to all cases.

of authority in making arrests, but zero immunity from being arrested.

If you are arrested, don't say anything. Call the bondsman that hired you and attempt to get bail and start your defense.

The first thing you will have to do is gather cases that justify whatever you were just arrested for. Your attorney will research all laws that would indicate to a judge or jury that you acted within your area of authority. He will look at weapons laws: concealed, use in arrest, brandishing, shooting in self-defense, and so on. He'll point to anything that will protect you.

Appendices A, B, and C are three studies that are used quite often by attorneys in the defense of their bounty-hunter clients. These studies are well done, authoritative, and full of good case law that will cover most arrests of a bounty hunter.

CHAPTER FOURTEEN

National Association of Bail Enforcement Agents

Several years ago, the National Association of Bail Enforcement Agents was formed to enable bail enforcement agents to network, share information about the trade, and become more efficient. This was difficult to do, as there was no central registry to begin with. To date, it is the only organization for professional bail enforcement agents, having more than one hundred members. Remember, there are not that many *full-time* bail enforcement agents, so having as many members as they do is quite a coup. There are also several dozen bail-bond agents and two surety insurance companies as members.

The Association helps members with legal problems and has a enormous collection of legal documents regarding the trade that is shared with all members. It conducts ongoing research on legal matters concerning bail enforcement in order to stay up-to-date. If you are a working professional and would like to join, send a self-addressed, stamped envelope to the following address and request an application for membership:

NABEA
P.O. Box 3990
Santa Barbara, CA 93130

NABEA CODE OF ETHICS

As a member of the National Association of Bail Enforcement Agents, we pledge . . .

To perform all bail fugitive investigations in a moral, ethical, and legal manner.

To arrest the bail fugitive in the most humane, legal, and responsible manner possible.

To work entirely within the framework of the law: federal, state, and local.

To verify all paperwork, warrants, and documents which might lead to a wrongful arrest or detention.

To act in a fashion to bring credit to the bail bond industry, the bail agency we represent, and our association.

To report all facts developed in a case promptly and timely in order to assist in the bail agent's exoneration of bail.

To treat the prisoner in a humane, respectful, and nondegrading fashion while he or she is in our custody.

To aid the National Association of Bail Enforcement Agents in furthering the image of the bail bond industry and its agents and employees.

APPENDIX A

The Bondsman's Right to Arrest

Inspector Charles A. Donelan
Federal Bureau of Investigation
Washington, D.C.

An odd byway of arrest law which arouses the curiosity of the professional law enforcement officer is the right of a bondsman to arrest a person who has been admitted to bail pending trial. The reason it stirs his interest is plain, for in the words of the Supreme Court of the United States:

> No right is held more sacred, or is more carefully guarded, by the common law, than the right of every individual to the possession and control of his own person, free from all restraint or interference, unless by clear and unquestioned authority of law.[1]

To find the origin and nature of the bondsman's right to arrest under authority of law, we must go back, as in so many other aspects of arrest law, to the common law of England.[2]

PURPOSE OF BAIL

The principle of bail is basic to our system of justice and its practice as old as English law itself. When the administration of criminal justice was in its infancy, arrest for serious crime meant imprisonment without preliminary hearing and long periods of time could occur between apprehension and the arrival of the King's Justices to hold court. It was therefore a matter of utmost importance to a person under arrest to be able to obtain a provisional release from custody until his case was called.

This was also the *desideratum* of the medieval sheriff, the local representative of the Crown in criminal matters, who wore many hats, including that of bailing officer.

He preferred the conditional release of persons under arrest to their imprisonment for several reasons. For example, it was less costly and troublesome; the jails were easy to breach and under then existing law the jailer was hanged if a prisoner escaped;[3] the jails were dangerous to health and, as there was no provision for adequate food, many prisoners perished before trial was held.[4]

Influenced by factors such as these, the sheriff was inclined to discharge himself of responsibility for persons awaiting trial by handing them into the personal custody of their friends and relatives. Indeed, in its strict sense, the word "bail" is used to describe the person who agrees to act as surety for the accused on his release from jail and becomes responsible for his later appearance in court at the time designated.[5] As surety, the bail was liable under the law for any default in the accused's appearance.

Between the thirteenth and fifteenth centuries, the sheriff's power to admit bail was gradually vested, by a series of statutes, in the justices of the peace.

In the case of a person committed for felony, the justices of the peace had authority to require, if they thought fit, his remaining in jail until the trial took place; but, on the other hand, a person committed for trial in a misdemeanor case could, through common law, insist on being released on bail if he found sufficient sureties.[6]

Writing in the mid-1700s, Sir William Blackstone described the arrest bail procedure of his day in the following passage:

> When a delinquent is arrested . . . he ought regularly to be carried before a justice of the peace . . . If upon inquiry it manifestly appears that either no such crime was committed or that the suspicion entertained of the prisoner was wholly groundless, in such cases only it is lawful totally to discharge him. Otherwise he must either be committed to prison or give bail; that is, put in securities for his appearance to answer the charge against him. This commitment, therefore, being only for safe custody, wherever bail will answer the same intention it ought to be taken . . . Bail is . . . a delivery or bailment of a person to his sureties, upon their giving (together with himself) sufficient security for his appearance; he being supposed to continue in their friendly custody instead of going to gaol.[7]

The notion of bail pending trial has not changed over the centuries. For instance, Mr. Justice Robert H. Jackson of the Supreme Court, in discussing its purpose said:

> The practice of admission to bail, as it evolved in Anglo-American law, is not a device for keeping persons in jail upon mere accusation until it is found convenient to give them a trial. On the contrary, the spirit of the procedure is to enable them to stay out of jail until a trial has found them guilty. Without this conditional privilege, even those wrongfully accused are punished by a period of imprisonment while awaiting trial and are handicapped in consulting counsel, searching for evidence and witnesses, and preparing a defense . . . Admission to bail always involves a risk that the accused will take flight. That is a calculated risk which the

> law takes as the price of our system of justice.[8]

The possibility that the accused may flee or hide must, of course, be squared with the traditional right to freedom of pending trial. In order to reconcile these conflicting interests, therefore, his release on bail is conditioned upon his giving reasonable assurance in one form or another that he will appear at a certain time to stand trial. In this regard, the Supreme Court has remarked:

> Like the ancient practice of securing the oaths of responsible persons to stand as sureties for the accused, the modern practice of requiring a bail bond or the deposit of a sum of money subject to forfeiture serves as an additional assurance of the presence of the accused.[9]

Modern statutes, which regulate bail procedure in detail today, and vary from jurisdiction to jurisdiction, provide that an accused may be set at liberty pending trial in several ways.[10]

For example, he may be released without security by agreeing in writing to appear at a specified time and place, i.e., "on his own recognizance;"[11] or he may execute a bond with a deposit of cash or securities in an amount equal to or less than the face amount of the bond; or he may execute a bail bond which requires one or more sureties.

THE BAIL BOND

A bail bond, with sureties, is essentially a contract between the government on the one side and the accused and his sureties on the other. Under the contract the accused is released into the custody of the sureties on their promise to pay the government a stated sum of money if the accused fails to appear before the court in accordance with its terms.

Historically, the contract of bail, traced to a gradual

increase of faith in the honor of the hostage and the consequent relaxation of actual imprisonment, constitutes one of the first appearances of the concept of contract in our law.[12]

The early contract of bail differed from the modern bail bond in its mode of execution, as it was simply a solemn admission of liability by the sureties made in the presence of an officer authorized to take it. No signature of the bail was required and it was not necessary for the person bailed to bind himself as a party. The undertaking to forfeit a particular sum in a written bail bond came later in the course of time.[13]

The purpose of a bail bond with sureties is to insure that the accused will appear in court at a given time by requiring others to assume responsibility for him on penalty of forfeiture of their property. In times past, especially when the sureties were friends and relatives of the accused, it was assumed that due to this personal relationship the threat of forfeiture of the sureties' property would serve as an effective deterrent to the accused's temptation to break the conditions of the bond by flight. On the other hand, it was assumed that this threat would also inspire the sureties to keep close watch on the accused to prevent his absconding.

On a bail bond, the accused and the sureties are the obligors, the accused being the principal, and the government is the obligee. In the event the conditions of the bail bond are satisfied, the obligation is void; the accused and sureties are exonerated and any cash or other securities deposited are returned to them. If there is a breach of the bail bond's conditions, however, the obligation remains in full force and the accused and his sureties are liable to the government for the sum stated. A forfeiture of the bond will be declared on default but in the interests of justice the forfeiture may be set aside or, if entered, its execution may be stayed or the penalty remitted.

For example, the surrender of the principal after forfeiture does not discharge the surety but nevertheless the court may receive the surrender and remit the penalty in whole or in part.

As in the past, the sureties on a bail bond in England are still the friends and relatives of the accused. Consequently the relationship between them remains personal and the accused's natural sense of moral obligation to satisfy the conditions of the bond is strong. As a result, the English experience has been, on the whole, that very few persons admitted to bail fail to appear for trial. In the United States, however, this close relationship has generally yielded to a distant impersonal connection and the moral obligation has become in the main a financial one. More often than not the sureties on a bail bond are surety companies and professional bail bondsmen who operate on a broad scale and charge fees for their services which may not only be large but also irretrievable regardless of whether the accused appears.

Under the traditional view taken in England, bail is not a mere contract of suretyship and the accused is not allowed to indemnify the bail.[14] In fact, it has been held that any arrangement between the accused and his sureties to the effect that he will indemnify them if he absconds is so contrary to public policy that it is void as an agreement and, moreover, is indictable as a conspiracy to pervert the course of justice.[15] This view contrasts with that taken in the United States, where an express agreement by the principal to indemnify his surety in a criminal case since it would destroy the effective safeguards provided by the interested watchfulness of the bail. Mr. Justice Oliver Wendell Holmes stated:

> [T]he ground for declaring the contract invalid rests rather on tradition than on substantial realities of the present day. It is said that ... nothing should be done to diminish the interest of the bail in producing

> the body of his principal. But bail no longer is the "mundium," although *a trace of the old relation remains in the right to arrest.* The distinction between bail and suretyship is pretty nearly forgotten. The interest to produce the body of the principal in court is impersonal and wholly pecuniary. If, as in this case, the bond was for $40,000, that sum was the measure of the interest on anybody's part and it did not matter to the Government what person ultimately felt the loss so long as it had the obligation it was content to take.[16] (Emphasis added by writer.)

Despite the tenor of the foregoing passage, courts still stress the need for a moral as well as financial assurance of the accused's appearance in court. For example, in a case where the bail offered was a certified check from an individual, the Federal Court of Appeals for the Second Circuit, in requiring disclosure of the source of funds on which the check was drawn, declared:

> The giving of security is not the full measure of the bail's obligation. It is not the sum of the bail bond that society asks for, but rather the presence of the defendant . . . If the court lacks confidence in the surety's purpose or ability to secure the appearance of a bailed defendant, it may refuse its approval of a bond even though the financial standing of the bail is beyond question.[17]

ORIGIN, BASIS, AND SCOPE OF RIGHT TO ARREST

What is the origin and basis in the law for the bondsman's right to arrest a person admitted to bail pending trial? In, as Mr. Justice Holmes stated, this "trace of the old relation" between accused and surety which still remains.

It is bottomed on the common law principle that the accused is transferred to the friendly custody of his sureties and is at liberty only by their permission.

At the time of the Norman Conquest of England, sureties for the accused were compared to his jailers and were said to be the "Duke's living person."[18] This relationship between them has been described in the cases since those days in like picturesque language. For example, it has been said: "[T]he principal is, in the theory of the law, committed to the custody of the sureties as to jailers of his own choosing;"[19] and "the bail have their principal on a string and may pull the string whenever they please."[20]

Thus, in legal contemplation, when the accused is released on bail, his body is deemed to be delivered to his sureties. The contract of bail "like debt as dealt with by the Roman law of the Twelve Tables . . . looked to the body of the contracting party as the ultimate satisfaction."[21]

In early times, bail implied a stringent degree of custodial responsibility[22] and the sanction of the law for any failure on the part of the sureties was harsh. When the accused was released on bail, he and his sureties were said to be bound "body for body." As late as the fourteenth century, an English judge, after noting that bail were the accused keeper's, declared that it had been maintained that if the accused escaped, the bail would be hanged in his place.[23] But, on the other hand, it seems that during the previous century, sureties who failed to produce their man in court got off with a fine, all their chattels theoretically being at the King's mercy.

In a modern case, the responsibility of the sureties has been described as follows: "If the defendant had been placed in jail, he could have been brought into court for trial. The bondsmen are as the four walls of the jail, and 'in order to fully discharge their obligations they are obliged to secure their principal's presence and put him as much in the power of the court as if he were in the custody of the proper officer.' "[24]

As to the modern sanction of the law, of course, if the accused flees and fails to appear in court at the required time, the bail bond is forfeited and surety is absolutely liable to the government as a debtor for the full amount of the penalty.

With such a stern responsibility of safekeeping to insure that the accused answered the call of the court, it followed in reason that the law would afford the means to carry it out, as the practical common law did, by recognizing a right of arrest in the bondsman. Although the right arises from the theory of the sureties' custody, i.e., the principal is "so far placed in their power that they may at any time arrest him upon the recognizance and surrender him to the court"[25] for exoneration—it also bears a resemblance to the right of arrest which existed under the medieval frankpledge system of law enforcement. That system, designed to keep the King's Peace, was one of mutual suretyship, with each man responsible for the good conduct of the other nine members of his tithing and with each having the duty to aid in the capturing of fugitives from justice. The resemblance is close, for up to the early decades of the thirteenth century, prisoners were often handed over to a tithing and sometimes a whole township was made responsible for their appearance before the court.[26]

The scope of the bondsman's right to arrest the accused, based on the metaphysical link that binds them, was viewed by the U.S. Supreme Court in the course of its opinion in the interesting case of *Taylor v. Taintor*.[27]

In this case, which is discussed below, the Court said:

> When bail is given, the principal is regarded as delivered to the custody of his sureties. Their dominion is a continuance of the original imprisonment. Whenever they choose to do so, they may seize him and deliver him up in their discharge and if that

> cannot be done at once, they may imprison him until it can be done. They may exercise their rights in person *or by agent*. They may pursue him into another state; may arrest him on the Sabbath; and if necessary, may break and enter his house for that purpose. The seizure is not made by virtue of new process. None is needed. It is likened to the rearrest, by the sheriff, of an escaping prisoner."[28] (Emphasis added.)

As to the above-mentioned right of surety to arrest by means of an agent, it has been held[29] that the surety, in the absence of statutory limitations, may deputize others of suitable age and discretion to take the prisoner into custody, but the latter authority may not be delegated. Where a statute provides the manner in which the power of arrest may be delegated by the bail bondsman, that provision must be followed or the rearrest is invalid. In some jurisdictions, a statute provides for an arrest by the sheriff on a direction of the bail endorsed on a certified copy of the recognizance. Where the surety on a bail bond procures the rearrest of his principal by a sheriff, or other peace officer, it is the general rule that the officer is empowered to make the arrest as an agent of the surety and not an officer "per se." Where a statute prescribes the formalities to be followed before an arrest may be made by a peace officer as agent of a surety, compliance with the statute is necessary for a lawful arrest.

As to the above-mentioned right of a surety to pursue his principal into another state, it has been held[30] that, just as the surety can arrest and surrender the principal without resort to legal process when the latter remains within the jurisdiction, he can pursue him into another state to arrest him, detain him, and return him to the state whence he fled and where the bail bond was executed and his presence is required. A surety has the right at any time to discharge himself from liability by surrendering the principal before the bail bond is forfeited, and can arrest him for that purpose. His right to seize and surrender the principal is an original right, not a right derived through the state, which arises from the undertaking in the bail bond and the relationship between principal and bail. It is a private right and not a matter of criminal procedure; jurisdiction does not enter into the question and there is no obstacle to its exercise wherever the surety finds the principal. The surety's right in such a case differs from that of the state which desires to reclaim a fugitive from its justice in another jurisdiction.

In default of a voluntary return, the state can remove a defendant from another state only by the process of extradition and must proceed by way of extradition which can only be exercised by a government at the request of a government.

The case of *Taylor v. Taintor*,[31] noted above, which was decided by the Supreme Court in 1873, dealt with the problems raised by the interstate travel of the principal on a bail bond and liabilities of the surety in that regard. The holding of the Court was that where a principal was allowed by his bail to go into another state and, while there, was delivered upon a requisition from a third state upon a criminal charge committed in that state, such proceedings did not exonerate the bail.

The case arose in the following manner:

A man named McGuire was charged, by information, with the crime of grand larceny in Connecticut and arrested upon a bench warrant. The court fixed the amount of bail to be given at $8,000. McGuire was released from custody on a bail bond in that sum, with two sureties, conditioned that he appear before the court on a set day the following month. After his release on bond, McGuire went to New York where he lived. While he was there, however, he was seized by New York officers upon the strength of a requisition made upon the Governor of New York by the Governor of Maine, charging McGuire with a burglary, alleged to have been committed by him in the latter state before the Connecticut bail bond was taken.

Subsequently, McGuire was delivered to Maine officers who removed him against his will to that state where he was later tried and convicted on the burglary charge.

When, due to the New York arrest and removal, McGuire failed to appear before the Connecticut court on the appointed day, his bail bond was forfeited. Neither of his sureties knew when they entered on the bond that there was any criminal charge against McGuire other than the Connecticut grand larceny. The treasurer of the State of Connecticut successfully sued to recover the amount of the obligation of the bail bond and the state high court and ultimately the Supreme Court of the United States affirmed the judgment.

In their effort to resist the forfeiture, the sureties contended that it was impossible for them to produce McGuire before the Connecticut court pursuant to the condition of the bail bond since he had been arrested in New York and removed to Maine by force of the Constitution of the United States and the interstate rendition laws enacted by Congress. To this contention the Supreme Court replied that the failure of McGuire to appear was caused by the supineness and neglect of the sureties, not the Constitution and laws of the United States, and held, accordingly, that they were not entitled to exoneration.

In reaching this conclusion, the Court declared at the outset that according to settled law the sureties will be exonerated when the performance of the condition of a bail bond is rendered impossible by the act of God, the act of the obligee, or the act of the law. On the other hand, it is equally settled that if the impossibility is created by the sureties, the rights of the State are in no way affected.

As to exoneration by "the act of the law," the Court explained, the sureties will be exonerated if the principal is arrested in the state where the obligation is given and is sent out of that state by the Governor upon the requisition of the Governor of another state. In doing so, the Governor represents the sovereignty of the state; the state can no longer require the court; and the obligation it has taken to secure his appearance loses its binding effect.

But if the principal is imprisoned in another state for the violation of a criminal law of that state, the principal and his sureties will not be protected. The law which renders the performance impossible, and therefore excuses failure, must be a law operative in the state where the obligation was assumed and which is obligatory in its effect upon her authorities. The Court stated that where a demand is properly made by the Governor of one state upon the Governor of another, the duty to surrender a fugitive is not absolute and unqualified. It depends upon the circumstances of the case. If the laws of the latter state have been put in force against the fugitive, and he is imprisoned there, the demands of those laws may first be satisfied. The Court noted that bail may doubtless permit the principal to go beyond the limits of the state within which he is to answer. But it is unwise and imprudent to do so because if any evil ensues, the bail must bear the burden of the consequences and cannot cast them upon the state.

After laying out the foregoing principles, the Court declared that the sureties in this case were not entitled to be exonerated because:

1. When the Connecticut bail bond was forfeited for the nonappearance of McGuire, the action of the Governor of New York, pursuant to the requisition of the Governor of Maine, had spent its force and had come to an end. McGuire was then held in custody under the law of Maine to answer to a criminal charge pending there against him, a fact which, as explained above, cannot avail the sureties.

2. If McGuire had remained in Connecticut, he would probably not have been delivered over to the Maine authorities and would not have been disabled to fulfill the condition of his obligation. If the demand had been made upon the Governor of Connecticut, he might properly have declined to comply until the criminal justice of his own state had been satisfied. It is not to be doubted that he would have exercised this right, but had he failed to do so, the obligation of the bail bond would have been released. But here, the sureties were at fault for McGuire's departure from Connecticut and they must take the consequences. Indeed, their fault reached further for, having permitted McGuire to go to New York, it was their duty to be aware of his arrest when it occurred and to interpose their claim to his custody.
3. When McGuire was arrested in New York, the original imprisonment under the Connecticut information was continued. The bail had a right to seize him wherever they could find him. The prosecution in Connecticut was still pending and its court's jurisdiction could not be suspended by any other tribunal. Though he was beyond the jurisdiction of Connecticut, McGuire was still, through his bail, in the hands of the law of that state and held to answer for the offense with which he was charged. Had the facts been made known to the Governor of New York by the sureties at the proper time, it is to be presumed that he would have ordered McGuire to be delivered to them and not to the authorities of Maine.
4. The act of the Governor of New York in making the surrender was not "the act of the law" within the legal meaning of those terms. In the view of the law, it was the act of McGuire himself. He violated the law of Maine and thus put in motion the machinery provided to bring him within the reach of the punishment for his offense. But for this, such

machinery, so far as he was concerned, would have remained dormant. McGuire cannot be allowed to avail himself of an impossibility of performance thus created. What will not avail him cannot avail his sureties. His contract is identical with theirs. They undertook for him what he undertook for himself.

5. The constitutional provision and the law of Congress, under which the arrest and delivery of McGuire to Maine were made, are obligatory upon every state and are a part of the law of every state. Every Governor, however, acts separately and independently for himself. In the event of refusal, the state making the demand must submit. There is no alternative. But in McGuire's case no impediment appeared to the Governor of New York and he properly yielded obedience. The Governor of Connecticut, if applied to, might have rightfully postponed compliance. If advised in season he might have intervened and by a requisition have asserted the claim of Connecticut. It would then have been for the Governor of New York to decide between the conflicting demands.

The Court concluded by noting that the State of Connecticut was not in any sense a party to what was done in New York and that if McGuire had been held in custody in New York at the time fixed for his appearance in Connecticut, it would not in any way have affected the obligation of the bail bond.

STATUTES DECLARATORY OF COMMON LAW RIGHT

Modern statutes provide for the right of surety to arrest an accused released on a bail bond, thus preserving by legislation the authority first granted by the medieval common law. Under the Federal statute declaratory of this right,[32] any accused charged with a criminal offense who is released on a bail bond with sureties may be arrested by the surety, delivered to the U.S. Marshal, and brought before any judge or officer empowered to commit for such offense.

At the request of the surety, such judicial officers may recommit the accused to the custody of the marshal and endorse on the bond the discharge and exonerator of the surety. Thereafter the accused may be held in custody until discharged in due course of law.

In regard to the bondsman's ancient right to arrest, it is noted that when the State of Illinois enacted new bail statutes in 1963, aimed at rectifying abuses of the professional bail bondsman system and reducing the cost of liberty to accused persons awaiting trial, the primary argument advanced in favor of retaining the system was that the bondsman would, at his own expense, track down and recapture a defendant who jumped bail. The Illinois Legislature, however, found that this argument had only tenuous support, as its "Committee Comments" included the following statement:

> As to the value of bondsmen being responsible for the appearance of the accused and tracking him down and returning him at the bondsman's expense—the facts do not support this as an important factor. While such is accomplished occasionally without expense to the county, the great majority of bail jumpers are apprehended by the police of this and other states . . .[33]

BAIL JUMPING STATUTES

The penalties of the common law designed to ensure the appearance in court of an accused out on bail and to deter him from absconding were limited to forfeiture of the bail bond and contempt of court.[34]

These traditional sanctions, however, have been supplemented and bolstered in some jurisdictions through the power of the criminal law by legislative enactment of so-called bail jumping statutes.[35] Under these laws, the accused is subjected to the criminal punishments of fine and imprisonment for breaching the conditions of his release by willful failure to appear. Such statutes are of comparatively recent vintage. For example, the New York law, said to be the first in the country, was passed in 1928, and the Federal statute was enacted in 1954.[36]

The purpose of these penal laws is to improve the administration of justice by creating a personal deterrent to the flight of those who may prefer to forfeit bail; for example, those who desire to purchase their freedom for the price of the bail bond or those who feel no financial deterrent as they expect the ultimate loss to fall on impersonal sureties.

Under these statutes aimed at the bail jumper, the general elements are: That a person has been admitted to bail; that he willfully failed to appear as required; that the forfeiture of his bail has been incurred by reason of his failure to appear; and that he did not appear and surrender himself within the specified period after the forfeiture. The offense may be a felony or misdemeanor in grade, depending upon that of the original offense for which the bail was given. Thus, the Federal statute provides that anyone released on bond who willfully fails to appear as required shall incur a forfeiture of any security given or pledged for his release. In addition, if he was released in connection with a charge of felony, he shall be fined not more than $5,000 or imprisoned not more than five years or both. If he was released in connection with a charge of misdemeanor, he shall be fined not more than the maximum provided for such misdemeanor or imprisoned for not more than one year or both.

CONCLUSION

Since the flight of the accused condemned by the bail-jumping statutes is a criminal offense, the offender is subject to arrest by the professional law enforcement officer just like any other person who violates the penal code of the jurisdiction. But whether the arrest of a person released on bail, who willfully fails to appear in court when required, is made by an officer of the law pursuant to the provisions of the foregoing type of criminal statute, or under the traditional command of the court, or is effected by a bondsman under his ancient right of arrest at common law, the apprehension of the absconder serves the same vital end. Like any proper arrest, it is the initial essential step in the administration of justice ultimately "intended to vindicate society's interest in having its laws obeyed."[37]

ENDNOTES

1. Union Pac. R.R., *Co. v. Botsford*, 141 U.S. 250, 251 (1891).
2. *See* Stephen, *A History of the Criminal Law of England*, 233-234; Orfield, *Criminal Procedure from Arrest to Appeal*, 101-134; 8 C.J.S., Bail, 87; 8 Am. Jur. 2d, *Bail and Recognizance*, 114-119; 3 A.L.R. 186, 73, 1370.
3. Holmes, *The Common Law*, 249-250.
4. *Kenny's Outlines of Criminal Law* (18th ed.), 571.
5. The term "bail" has other meanings. For example, it is used to refer to the security or obligation assumed by the surety and, as a verb, to signify the delivery of an arrested person to his sureties. See 8 C.J.S., Bail 1.
6. Kenny, *supra*, 119.
7. 4 Blackstone, Com. (1769) 296.
8. *Stock v. Boyle*, 342 U.S. 1, 7-8 (1951).
9. *Stock v. Boyle, supra*, 5 (1951).
10. *See*, for illustration, rule 46, *Federal Rules of Criminal Procedure*, and 18 U.S. Codes 3146.
11. The words "recognizance" and "bail bond" are not synonymous in the law but they are often used interchangeably, as they both constitute obligations with the same purpose, i.e., the accused's appearance in court is the condition of nonforfeiture.
12. Holmes, *supra*, 249-250.
13. Pollock & M., *History of English Law*, 587-588.
14. *See* Orfield, *supra*; Kenny, *supra*, 571-572.
15. Kenny, *supra*, 571-572.
16. *Leary v. United States*, 224 U.S. 567, 575-576 (1912).
17. *United States v. Nebbia*, 357 F. 2d 303, 304 (1966).
18. Pollock & M., *supra*, 587.
19. *Reese v. United States*, 9 Wall. (U.S.) 13, 21 (1870).
20. *See Taylor v. Taintor*, 16 Wall. (U.S.) 366, 372 (1873) quoting old English decision.

21. Holmes, *supra*, 249-250.
22. 2 Pollock & M., *supra*, 587.
23. Holmes, *supra*, 249-250.
24. *Roberts v. State*, 32 Ga. App. 339, 341 (1924).
25. *Reese v. United States*, *supra*, 21.
26. 2 Pollock & M., *supra*, 587-588.
27. *Taylor v. Taintor*, 16 Wall. (U.S.) 366 (1873).
28. *Id.* at 371-372.
29. *See* 8 Am. Jur. 2d, *Bail and Recognizance*, 115; Anno: 3 A.L.R. 186; 8 C.J.S., *Bail*, 87 c.
30. *Fitzpatrick v. Williams*, 46 F. 2d 40 (1931).
31. *See supra* note 20.
32. 18 U.C.S. 3142.
33. *See* note 3 to dissenting opinion of Mr. Justice Douglas in *Schilb v. Kuebel*, 30 L. Ed. 2d 502 (1971).
34. *See* 18 U.S.C. 3151: *Brown v. United States*, 410 F. 2d 212 (1969); *United States v. Green*, 241 F. 2d 631 (1956).
35. *See* Orfield, *supra*; 8 C.J.S., *Bail*, 51 (2).
36. *See* 18 U.S.C. 3150; 18 U.S.C. 3146.
37. *Terry v. Ohio*, 392 U.S. 1, 26 (1968).

APPENDIX B

The Hunters and the Hunted: Rights and Liabilities of Bail Bondsmen

Fordham Urban Law Journal
Volume VI, Number 2

INTRODUCTION

For over 150 years, bail bondsmen have had the right to arrest their principals[1] whenever and wherever they chose, and to recommit them to government custody in order to avoid forfeiture of their bond.[2] This right was upheld when a bail bondsman forcibly entered his principal's home in the middle of the night,[3] when the bondsman pursued his principal beyond state lines,[4] and even when the bondsman used physical force in the act of apprehension.[5]

This Note will examine the development of this extrajudicial power to make arrests, the manner in which it is handled in the context of tort law, and the impact of civil rights legislation on the rights of bail bondsmen.

BAIL BONDSMEN IN THE NINETEENTH CENTURY

As early as 1810, *Nicolls v. Ingersoll*[6] established the bail bondsman's right, independent of government authority, to arrest his principal at any time before or after a scheduled court appearance. The New York court describing this power stated:

> The power of taking and surrendering is not exercised under any judicial process, but results from the nature of the undertaking by the bail. The bail piece is not process, nor anything in the nature of it, but is merely a record or memorial of the delivery of the principal to his bail, on security given ... [T]his shows that the jurisdiction of the court in no way controls the authority of the bail; and as little can the jurisdiction of the State affect this right, as between the bail and his principal.[7]

Besides establishing that bail bondsmen derive their power of arrest not from the State, but from the private contractual relationship between bondsman and principal, *Nicolls v. Ingersoll* also established the right of the bondsmen to appoint agents to make such arrests.[8] The *Nicolls* Court stated that it saw "nothing on general principles, against allowing this power to be exercised by an agent or deputy, and no case is to be found where the right has been denied."[9] In addition, the court in *Nicolls* propounded the doctrine that bondsmen could pursue and arrest a fugitive principal anywhere within the state or nation.[10] It likewise refused to disturb the jury's finding that the apprehension was not accomplished by means of unreasonable force.

Plaintiff Nicolls had been released on a $500 bond in Connecticut.[11] Before Nicolls' scheduled appearance, the bondsman authorized his agent, the defendant, to cross into New York and arrest Nicolls.[12] After being denied entry into plaintiff Nicolls' house, the defendant broke into the house about midnight.[13] With the aid of two companions the defendant roused Nicolls from his bed, took him "with great roughness" without his coat, and transported him to Connecticut.[14]

Nicolls sued the bondsman's agent in tort for trespass, false imprisonment, and assault and battery.[15] The jury found for the defendant and the New York court accepted without question the jury's finding of fact that the defendant did not use unreasonable force in arresting Nicolls.[16] *Nicolls* thus gave bondsmen wide latitude in choosing when, where, and how to apprehend their principals. The *Nicolls* Court termed these rights "indispensable for the safety and security of bail."[17]

Twelve years after *Nicolls*, a similar situation arose in *Read v. Case*. As in *Nicolls*, the bondsman employed an agent to make the arrest.[19] The agent broke into the plaintiff's home, struck him, and imprisoned him.[20]

The *Read* Court, while finding for the defendant bondsman, was more explicit than *Nicolls* in stating what a bail bondsman could and could not do in arresting his principal. The court stated that before a bondsman or his agent could break into a principal's house to make an arrest, the bondsman or agent must announce his identity and intention.[21] If peaceful entry is denied it would then be lawful to break in and make the arrest.[22] Although the bondsman's agent made no such announcement before breaking into the plaintiff's house, the *Read* Court excused this omission because the plaintiff had declared that he would meet with force any such attempt to take him.[23] The court decided that "[I]t would be a palpable perversion of a sound rule to extend the benefit of it to a man, who had full knowledge of the information he insists should have been communicated; and who waited only for a demand, to wreak on his bail the most brutal and unhallowed vengeance."[24]

Thus the court in *Read* essentially agreed with the *Nicolls* holding but articulated in greater detail and with greater emphasis the restriction on bail bondsmen that the *Nicolls* Court briefly noted.[25] That common law requirement emerged early as one small check on the broad powers of bail bondsmen.

It was not until 1869 that the United States Supreme Court dealt with the rights of bail bondsmen. In *Reese v. United States*,[26] the Court stated that a bail bondsman may arrest his principal anywhere in the country and may do whatever is necessary to capture and return him to custody.[27] The *Reese* Court also referred to the private contractual nature of the bail-principal relationship in stating that the government impliedly covenanted not to interfere in any way with this right of the bondsman.[28] Such language from the highest court in the land amounted to nothing less than a carte blanche to bail bondsmen to take whatever liberties they felt were necessary in arresting their principals.

The Supreme Court decision in *Taylor v. Taintor*[29] soon gave further encouragement to bail bondsmen. Unlike *Nicolls* and *Read*, *Taylor* was not a tort action brought by a principal against his bondsman.[30] However, the Court did expound on the nature of the bondsman-principal relationship and the rights of the parties. The Court aptly described the power of the bondsman over his principal: "The bail have their principal on a string, and may pull the string whenever they please, and render him in their discharge."[31] The Court further asserted that no right of the state was involved[32] nor was any judicial process necessary for the bail to assert his "dominion" over the principal.[33]

The *Taylor* Court also affirmed the right of a bondsman to authorize agents to arrest his principal for him[34] and most significantly the Court reiterated the *Nicolls* and *Read* doctrine that a bondsman may, if necessary, break and enter his principal's home to arrest him.[35]

Twenty years later in *United States v. Keiver*,[36] the United States Circuit Court for the Western District of Wisconsin similarly held that a bondsman could seize his principal at any time and any place, including his home, which in the Anglo-American legal tradition, was a man's castle.[37]

The outer limits of the bondsman's rights were reached in *State v. Lingerfelt*,[38] decided in the late nineteenth century. A bondsman's agent shot and killed the bondsman's principal when the man resisted arrest with a farm implement.[39] The agent was convicted of murder.[40] On appeal the North Carolina Supreme Court reversed the conviction and granted a new trial.[41] The court decided that the trial court had construed the rights of a bondsman in rearresting his principal too restrictively. Citing *Taylor* and *Nicolls* as the correct rule of law,[42] the court indicated that under the broad powers granted to bail bondsmen, the defendant Lingerfelt may have been within his rights in using whatever force he felt was necessary to arrest the principal.[43]

The courts in the nineteenth century thus put few limits on the methods bail bondsmen could use in arresting their principals. The essential reason for judicial reluctance to interfere in this area was the private contractual nature of the bondsman-principal relationship from which the bondsman derived his sweeping power of arrest.[44] The essence of the contractual agreement was that the bondsman agreed to post bail for the principal in order that he (the principal) be freed temporarily from prison, pending resolution of the charges against him. In return the principal agreed that the bondsman could rearrest him whenever he chose, either before the principal was to appear in court or after he failed to do so. And as the Supreme Court stated in *Reese*, the government impliedly agreed not to interfere with the bondsman's right to safeguard his bond.[45]

Nor was process considered necessary for a bondsman to rearrest his principal.[46] Since no power of the state or federal government was involved, there was no need to comply with constitutional requirements of due process or equal protection of the laws.[47] The courts in the early cases did not apply these constitutional principles. In *In re Von Der Ahe* wherein plaintiff argued that his constitutional rights were violated,[48] the court rejected his claim of deprivation of liberty without due process of law, again holding that the private contract between bail and principal was beyond the boundaries of constitutional requirements.[49]

Aggrieved principals seeking redress against overzealous bondsmen and their agents have relied almost exclusively on the ordinary common law tort remedies for false imprisonment and assault and battery. As the cases reveal, the courts construe the bail contract to allow bondsmen wide discretion in how they conduct their business.[50] Thus, the tort approach had had little success.

THE DEVELOPMENT OF LIMITS ON THE RIGHTS OF BAIL BONDSMEN SINCE 1900

Adherence to the Nineteenth Century Doctrines

The decisions rendered during the first half of the twentieth century adhered closely to the holdings of the nineteenth century cases.[51]

One of the earlier cases in this century, *Fitzpatrick v. Williams*,[52] reaffirmed all the earlier common law principles which were so favorable to the bail bondsman. In restating the private contractual basis of the bail-principal relationship,[53] the United States Court of Appeals for the Fifth Circuit held that bail bondsmen had the right to arrest their principals without a warrant,[54] pursue them across state lines, return them to the home state without extradition proceedings,[55] authorize agents to make such arrests for them,[56] and essentially use any means necessary to effect such an arrest.[57] These basic tenets of the bail-principal relationship have been upheld in numerous cases.[58]

By the middle of the twentieth century there were few judicial restraints upon the activities of bail bondsmen. For example, in *State v. Liakas*,[59] the Supreme Court of Nebraska stated in dictum that the bail bondsman may "forcibly arrest" his principal and deliver him to the authorities in order to obtain exoneration from his bond.[60] And in *Golla v. State*,[61] the Supreme Court of Delaware upheld the right of a bondsman to pursue his principal anywhere in the United States and return him from an asylum state without extradition proceedings.

Development of Limits through the Tort Approach

Despite a general lack of success in the mid-nineteenth and early twentieth century attempts to obtain relief against bail bondsmen through tort remedies,[62] such attempts have continued. The results have varied, and the implications for the future are still unclear.

A possible trend toward stricter controls is detectable in *McCaleb v. Peerless Ins. Co.*, a decision of the United States District Court for the District of Nebraska.[63] Plaintiff McCaleb sued his bond company in tort for false imprisonment, illegal detention, and violation of his constitutional liberties.[64] McCaleb was arrested for traffic violations in Nebraska.[65] He obtained a $200 bond from the defendant bond company and thereupon fled to California.[66] The defendant's agent followed him to California, arrested him with the aid of a local bail bondsman, and then drove him handcuffed around the state for eighty hours.[67] When the defendant's agent finally returned McCaleb to Nebraska, he took title to McCaleb's car, apparently to reimburse the defendant bond company for its forfeited bond.[68] Instead of then turning the plaintiff over to the authorities, as was his duty under the bond, the agent ordered him to leave Nebraska immediately.[69]

Chief Judge Richard E. Robinson found the defendant liable in tort for false imprisonment and illegal detention.[70] He likewise found the arrest illegal and severely chastised the defendant for acting solely to protect itself financially and in circumvention of its legal duties.[71] In conclusion he stated: "This type of action will not be tolerated by this Court, and had this occurred with respect to a bond given before this Court, the defendant would be forever barred from writing a bail bond in this Court in the future."[72]

McCaleb represents a radical departure from the earlier

cases, which uniformly denied recovery to principals who may have been abused by their bondsmen.[73] It is the first reported case to hold that a bondsman had overstepped the limits of his authority and was therefore liable in tort to his principal. The very establishment of some limits, however vaguely defined, on the nearly unrestricted powers of bail bondsmen was a long overdue development in this field of law.

An even more important case in terms of what it said, if not for what it accomplished, is *Shine v. State*.[74] Apparently Shine owed the bond company $40 on a bond which it had written for him.[75] Consequently three men armed with pistols and shotguns were sent to Shine's house at 5:00 A.M. to arrest him.[76] When one of the men tried to break into the house, Shine shot and killed him.[77] The Alabama Appeals Court reversed Shine's conviction and granted a new trial.[78]

The court harshly condemned the tactics and intent (collection of a $40 debt) of the "armed posse."[79] It pointed out that bond companies have no right to arrest people for debts and certainly not at 5:00 A.M., armed with pistols and shotguns.[80] The court found that Shine had been justified in believing that his victim was not a law officer and therefore was under no obligation to surrender to him.[81] Legitimately thinking himself to be in danger of great bodily harm, he could be guilty of no greater crime than manslaughter.[82] The court then suggested that "[t]he controls over the bail should henceforth be tightened to exclude the use of weapons when not justified, to provide for investigation into every instance where it is claimed that weapons are needed, and the mandatory accompaniment by a law enforcement officer on such occasions."[83]

The decision of the court in *Shine* represents the strongest judicial attack to date on the liberties bail bondsmen are allowed to take with their principals. The Alabama Appeals Court not only condemned the methods used by bail bondsmen, but also emphatically advocated strong legislative action to place strict controls on the business. This call for legislative action was unprecedented.

The *McCaleb* and *Shine* decisions indicated a trend toward tighter controls on bail bondsmen. Yet in two subsequent cases, there appears to be a reversal of the trend and a return to the earlier lax attitude.

Six years after *Shine*, the Alabama Appeals Court had another opportunity to deal with the rights of bail bondsmen and their principals in *Livingston v. Browder*,[84] In this case the principal's mother sued the bondsman for having entered her property, albeit peacefully, to arrest her son.[85] The court held for the defendant and stated that a bondsman has the authority to enter the dwelling of a third party to arrest his principal if he knows the principal is in the dwelling, properly identifies himself, and uses reasonable means to gain entry.[86]

While the *Livingston* Court did articulate the applicable standards of conduct for a bail bondsman in arresting his principal, it did not add anything to the existing body of law. Instead, the court emphasized the strong public-policy reasons for protecting the bail-principal relationship and the necessity of giving bondsmen broad discretion in apprehending bail jumpers.[87]

The *Livingston* decision is most interesting for what it did not say. There is no mention whatsoever of the decision in *Shine v. State*,[88] which came from the same bench and strongly advocated stricter controls on the activities of bail bondsmen. Presented with a clear opportunity to reinforce the stance taken in *Shine*, the *Livingston* Court chose to retreat to the traditional common law principles which gave bondsmen "wide latitude . . . to arrest their principals."[89]

Soon after *Livingston*, in 1975, the Tennessee Supreme Court also took a step backward. In *Poteete v. Olive*,[90] the plaintiff sued his bail bondsman for false imprisonment, assault and battery.[91] While making the arrest the bondsman's agents beat and kicked the plaintiff and broke the plaintiff's leg.[92] Although the plaintiff was awarded several thousand dollars in damages,[93] the court did not base its decision on the agents' egregious assault. Rather it focused on their failure to present the plaintiff with a certified copy of the bond when they arrested him, as Tennessee law requires.[94]

The *Poteete* Court did not indicate that anything was wrong with the manner in which the arrest was effected and implied that had the bond been properly presented, the plaintiff could not have recovered.[95]

The current utility of the tort approach is therefore uncertain. The earlier lack of judicial receptiveness to tort claims appeared to be giving way to a more restrictive view of the rights of bail bondsmen. But subsequent cases reveal a reluctance to effect a fundamental widespread change and seem to indicate that a principal suing his bail bondsman in tort will continue to have difficulty in recovering for injuries inflicted by that bondsman.

Development of Limits through a Federal Statutory and Constitutional Approach

An alternative to the tort approach which has become increasingly popular in actions against abusive bail bondsmen is the use of constitutional principles and the federal Civil Rights Acts.[96] Again, results have varied, but this approach appears to offer a greater possibility of reducing abuses by bail bondsmen.

One of the most serious reported instances of abuse was described in *United States v. Trunko*.[97] In *Trunko*, a deputy sheriff, authorized by an Ohio bond company, tracked a bail jumper to Arkansas, arrested him, and returned him to Ohio.[98] In making the arrest, the defendant burst into the fugitive's house at night, awakened him from sleep, identified himself as a law officer from Ohio, handcuffed him, and then drove him nonstop back to Ohio.[99]

The deputy was indicted for violation of a 1909 civil rights statute which prohibits anyone from willfully depriving a person of his constitutional rights and privileges under color of state law.[100] The United States District Court for the Eastern District of Arkansas found that the defendant had acted under color of state law since he had identified himself as an Ohio law officer.[101] The court also decided that the fugitive was deprived of his constitutional rights.[102] However, it was ultimately decided that the defendant was innocent of the charges because he had not acted willfully in depriving the fugitive of his rights.[103]

The court, nevertheless, severely condemned the defendant's actions, describing them as "high-handed, unreasonable, and oppressive"[104] and further declaring that the "defendant's actions constituted an affront to the duly constituted authority of [the state and local governments] and were of a nature tending to bring law enforcement into disrepute."[105] While acquitting the defendant on possibly dubious grounds,[106] the district court emphatically criticized the violent tactics employed by the agent of the bail bondsman.[107]

Similarly, the decision in *Thomas v. Miller*[108] indicated a growing judicial disapproval of the methods used by bail bondsmen in arresting their principals, although the plaintiff in this civil case failed to recover. In *Thomas*, the plaintiff failed to appear for imprisonment following the denial of his appeal of a grand larceny conviction.[109] He thereupon fled from Tennessee to Ohio.[110] His bail bondsman tracked him to Ohio, arrested him, chained him hand and foot, and allegedly forced him to ride on the floor of his car during the drive back to Tennessee.[111]

Plaintiff sued in the United States District Court for the Eastern District of Tennessee, claiming damages against his bondsman for violation of the Civil Rights Act of 1871, which makes it an actionable civil wrong to deprive any person of his constitutional rights and privileges under the color of state law.[112] He made no tort claim.

The court dismissed the action because the defendant had not acted under color of state law.[113] Since the defendants "were acting by reason of a contractual relationship with him,"[114] the court could supply no remedy for the plaintiff.

The court agreed that plaintiff was treated "roughly"[115] and suggested that he might have a cause of action in state court for "cruel and inhuman treatment" during the trip from Ohio to Tennessee.[116] While not as far reaching as *McCaleb*, *Shine*,[117] or *Trunko*, the *Thomas* Court indicated that there are limits to how far a bail bondsman can go in apprehending fugitive principals. The court implied that those limits were exceeded and if the defendants were acting under color of state law, the plaintiff may have recovered.[118]

A year after *Thomas v. Miller* was decided, the United States District Court for the District of Minnesota dealt with a similar problem in *Curtis v. Peerless Ins. Co.*[119] Curtis also was returned to Tennessee from Minnesota after jumping bail on a drunk driving charge.[120] Although he was handcuffed for a short time, his arrest was peaceful, and the defendants carried no firearms.[121] Curtis sued for false imprisonment and deprivation of his civil rights, also under the Civil Rights Act of 1871.[122] The court acknowledged that an action for unlawful seizure was cognizable under those statutes.[123] Again, the missing element was action under color of state law. In this case the plaintiff himself had failed to allege that the defendants had acted under color of state law. Therefore the action for violation of the plaintiff's civil rights was dismissed.[124] The court reiterated that the private contractual bail-principal relationship permitted such an arrest and that no state action was involved.[125]

As in *Thomas*, the court in dictum dealt with the problem of abuses: "So long as the bounds of reasonable means needed to effect the apprehension are not transgressed, and the purpose of the recapture is proper in the light of the surety's undertaking, sureties will not be liable for returning their principals to proper custody."[126]

In *Curtis*, the bounds of reasonable means were not transgressed because the arrest was peaceful and the plaintiff was unharmed. The court rejected the plaintiff's allegation that the defendants were "malicious and wanton," but intimated that such a showing would make them liable.[127] Since the plaintiff was not harmed, the court did not have to delineate the "bounds of reasonable means." Consequently, no concrete standards can be derived from this decision. Nevertheless, the *Curtis* opinion is noteworthy for its assertion in dictum that there are limits to the power of bail bondsmen.

Another constitutional challenge to the rights of bail bondsmen was decided in *Smith v. Rosenbaum*,[128] Smith was out on bail when he was arrested on another charge. Under the terms of the bail contract, Smith had agreed that if he were arrested on another charge the bondsman could surrender him to the authorities and obtain exoneration of the bond.[129] The bondsman did surrender him in this manner, complying with Pennsylvania law, which requires the bondsman to obtain a certified copy of the bond from an officer of the court before making the arrest.[130]

As in *Curtis*, there was no mistreatment or physical abuse of the plaintiff. He merely charged that the act of obtaining a certified copy of the bond deprived him of his constitutional rights and privileges and he was therefore entitled to damages under the Civil Rights Acts.[131]

The court found that obtaining the certified copy of the bond constituted an act under color of state law because Pennsylvania law mandated this procedure.[132] However, the court concluded that neither the plaintiff's rights under the statute nor due process of law were violated.[133] Having agreed to the terms of the private bail contract, the plaintiff could not claim that his rights were violated when the defendants merely acted pursuant to the terms of that contract.[134]

Unlike the other cases brought under the Civil Rights Acts,[135] the *Smith* Court found that there was action under color of state law. The Pennsylvania law under which the bail bondsman acted is similar to statutes in a number of other states.[136] Nevertheless, the *Smith* decision is the first case to hold that the action of obtaining a certified copy of the bond is an action under color of state law for the purposes of the Civil Rights Acts. This decision established a major precedent for extending the concept of state action to included the activities of bail bondsmen and thus removing one of the major obstacles to recovery under the Civil Rights Acts.[137]

The Development of Limits through Procedural Requirements—Greater Controls in Some States

The traditional common law allowed the bail bondsman to arrest his principal without a warrant, a certified copy (usually by the court clerk) of the bond undertaking being sufficient evidence of the bondsman's contractual right to make the arrest.[138] Several states have codified this common law requirement.[139] Furthermore, since the *Nicolls*[140] and *Read*[141] decisions, a bondsman or his agent, when attempting to arrest a principal in a dwelling, is required to announce his identity and demand peaceful surrender before breaking in to make the arrest.

Even when confronting his principal in a public place, the bondsman (or his agent) is required to announce his identity and intention and present the principal with a copy of the bond.[142]

Texas has gone furthest in controlling the procedural aspects of bail bondsmen's activities. In *Austin v. Texas*,[143] the bondsman was convicted on a criminal charge of false imprisonment.[144] He had written a $5,000 bail bond for a principal who later jumped bail.[145] In rearresting his principal to avoid forfeiture of the bond, the bondsman, along with two private citizens, kicked in the man's door, wrestled him to the ground, and handcuffed him.[146] The bondsman had no arrest warrant as required by the Texas Criminal Code[147] for a non-peaceable seizure. His conviction was affirmed, the bondsman having failed to comply with the statutory mandate.[148]

Despite the court's failure to condemn the forcible nature of the arrest, it is clear that the statute provides certain safeguards. Requiring bondsmen to go before a judge or magistrate and justify the need for a warrant has the effect of putting bondsmen under greater judicial supervision. Their conduct would be subject to the same scrutiny that the courts give to government law enforcement agencies. Perhaps even more important, the courts would then be more likely to consider arrests made with such warrants to be under color of state law.[149] Accordingly, a major obstacle to a finding of civil rights violations would be eliminated.

Another state to enact strict legislation controlling bail bondsmen is California. Under the California statute,[150] a bail bondsman from another state seeking to arrest a fugitive bail jumper from that other state must file affidavits and appear at a hearing before a local magistrate.[151] If the magistrate decides that there is probable cause to believe the bail bondsman, a warrant for the fugitive's arrest is issued and he is brought before the magistrate, who sets a time and place for a hearing and advises the individual of his rights to counsel and to the production of evidence at the hearing.[152] If the magistrate is convinced that the suspect is a fugitive from bail, he will issue an order allowing the bondsman to return the fugitive to the jurisdiction from which he escaped.[153] Failure to comply with the statute is a misdemeanor.[154]

The California procedures, although not applicable to California bail jumpers, are a great improvement over the common law. Protection against mistaken identities, a chance for a fair hearing in open court with the benefit of counsel, and greater scrutiny of the activities of bail bondsmen are the results of this statute.[155] Indeed, there appears to be no reason why bail bondsmen should not be subject to the same requirements of due process as are all federal, state, and local law enforcement agencies.[156]

ENDNOTES

1. *Read v. Case*, 4 Conn, 166 (1822); *Nicolls v. Ingersoll*, 7 Johns. (N.Y.) 145 (1810).

2. In this area of the law, the principal is the party who has been arrested and is seeking release from prison pending his scheduled court appearance. The party that posts the required amount of bail is commonly called the bail bondsman and in older cases is often referred to simply as the bail or the surety.

When an arrest is made on the basis of a warrant, the amount of bail usually is set by the judge authorizing the warrant and is noted on the warrant. By posting the amount of the bond with the police officer in charge of the station house, it is possible for the accused to obtain pre-trial release. P. WICE, *FREEDOM FOR SALE*, 21 (1974) (hereinafter Wice).

When an arrest is made without a warrant, as most arrests are, the accused must wait to be arraigned, at which time the arraignment judge will set the amount of bail. A judicially fixed bail schedule, based on the offense for which the arrest was made, if often used to set the amount. WICE 22-23.

3. *Read v. Case*, 4 Conn. 166 (1822); *Nicolls v. Ingersoll*, 7 Johns.(N.Y.) 145 (1810).

4. *Fitzpatrick v. Williams*, 46 F 2d 40 (5th Cir. 1931); *Read v. Case*, 4 Conn. 166 (1822); *Nicolls v. Ingersoll*, 7 Johns. (N.Y.) 145 (1810).

5. *State v. Lingerfelt*, 109 N.C. 755, 14 S.E. 75 (1891) (principal shot by bondsman's agent); *Read v. Case*, 4 Conn. 166 (1822) (principal struck during arrest); *Nicolls v. Ingersoll*, 7 Johns. (N.Y.) 145 (1810) (principal treated with "great roughness" by bondsman's agents).

6. 7 Johns. (N.Y.) 145 (1810).

7. *Id.* at 154.

8. *Id.*

9. *Id.* This principle of law has allowed bail bondsmen to employ what are, in effect, bounty hunters. *See Taylor v. Taintor*, 83 U.S. (16 Wall.) 366, 371-72 (1873); *Reese v. United States*, 76 U.S. (9 Wall.) 13, 21-22 (1869); *In re Von Der Ahe*, 85 F. 959 (C.C.W.D. Pa. 1878); *State v. Lingerfelt*, 109 N.C. 775, 14 S.E. 75 (1891).

10. *Nicolls v. Ingersoll*, 7 Johns. (N.Y.) 145, 154 (1810).

11. *Id.* at 146.
12. *Id.*
13. *Id.* at 147.
14. *Id.* at 148.
15. *Id.* at 145.
16. *Id.* at 157. The court stated: "Whether the authority to arrest was not abused by the exertion of undue force, or unnecessary severity, has been decided by the jury in favor of the defendant. This was a matter of fact, proper to their determination, and was fairly submitted to them. The verdict, therefore, on this point, ought not to be disturbed."
17. *Id.* at 156.
18. 4 Conn. 166 (1822).
19. *Id.*
20. *Id.*
21. *Id.* at 170.
22. *Id.*
23. *Id.*
24. *Id.*
25. *See Nicolls v. Ingersoll*, 7 Johns. (N.Y.) at 156, where the court presumed that proper demand for entry was made before the defendant broke in. Given the fact of the plaintiff's threat, the court in *Read* made the correct decision. Even in the absence of a threat there will always be cases where the fugitive is truly a dangerous person warranting dispensing with the rule. However, bondsmen have shown no inclination to differentiate between traffic violators and armed felons when making arrests.
26. 76 U.S. (9 Wall.) 13 (1869). This was an action by the United States against a surety for forfeiture of a bond on an individual accused of land fraud. The accused was allowed to return to Mexico by the United States Attorney pending resolution of two civil cases involving the same facts. The accused's bondsman was not notified of this agreement. When the civil cases were decided against the accused and the criminal charges were brought against him, he failed to return from Mexico. The Supreme Court decided in favor of the bondsman, the government having interfered with the bondsman's right to protect his security.
27. *Id.* at 21.
28. *Id.* at 22.
29. 83 U.S. (16 Wall.) 366 (1873).
30. *Id.* at 367-369. Taylor involved an action by a bondsman to recover the amount of his bond from his principal, who had been arrested for grand larceny in Connecticut. The plaintiff had posted an $8,000 bond for the principal, whereupon the latter traveled to New York. In New York he was arrested by the local police at the request of the governor of Maine, in whose state he was wanted for burglary. He was tried, convicted, and imprisoned in Maine, causing the plaintiff to forfeit his bond in Connecticut. *Id.*
31. *Id.* at 371-372.

32. *Id.*
33. *Id.* at 371.
34. *Id.*
35. *Id.*
36. 56 F. 422 (C.C.W.D. 1893) (action by the federal government to obtain forfeiture of a bond).
37. *Id.* at 426. Accord, *State v. Dwyer,* 70 Vt. 96, 39 A. 629 (1897).
38. 109 N.C. 775, 14 S.E. 75 (1891).
39. *Id.* at 775, 14 S.E. 75 (1891).
40. *Id.*
41. *Id.* at 776, 14 S.E. at 77. The trial court charged the jury that as a matter of law there was no evidence that the defendant had any lawful authority to arrest the victim. *Id.*, 14 S.E. at 76.
42. *Id.* at 777-78, 14 S.E. at 76-77.
43. *Id.* at 779, 14 S.E. at 77.
44. *See* note 9 *supra.*
45. 76 U.S. (9 Wall.) at 22.
46. *Taylor v. Taintor,* 83 U.S. (16 Wall.) 366, 371-72 (1873); In *re Von Der Ahe,* 85 F. 959, 960-63 (C.C.W.D. Pa. 1898); *Nicolls v. Ingersoll,* 7 Johns. (N.Y.) 145, 154 (1810); *State v. Lingerfelt,* 109 N.C. 775, 777-78, 14 S.E. 75, 76 (1891).
47. U.S. CONST., amends. V and XIV.
48. In *re Von Der Ahe,* 85 F. 959 (C.C.W.D. Pa. 1898) (plaintiff claimed he was deprived of his liberty without due process of law).
49. *Id.* at 962-63.
50. *See* note 44 and accompanying text *supra.*
51. *See* text accompanying notes 6-50 *supra.*
52. 46 F. 2d 40 (5th Cir. 1931). The plaintiff was arrested in New Orleans on charges of being a fugitive from justice in the state of Washington. Although these charges were dropped by the local authorities, a Washington bail company intervened and requested that the plaintiff be placed in its custody, presumably to obtain a discharge of the bond it had written for him. Plaintiff appealed the court's order that the sheriff accede to that request.
53. *Id.* at 40.
54. *Id.* at 41.
55. *Id.*
56. *Id.*
57. *Id.*
58. *See*, e.g., *Smith v. Rosenbaum,* 333 F. Supp. 35 (E.D. Pa. 1971), aff'd, 460 F. 2d 1019 (3rd Cir. 1972); *Curtis v. Peerless Ins. Co.*, 299 F. Supp. 429 (D. Minn. 1969); *Thomas v. Miller,* 282 F. Supp. 571 (E.D. Tenn. 1968); *McCaleb v. Peerless Ins. Co.*, 250 F. Supp. 512 (D. Neb. 1965).

To some extent these common law principles have been codified at 18 U.S.C. SS 3142 (1970), which provides that to discharge his obligation, a bail bondsman may arrest his principal at any time and deliver him to a federal marshal.

A number of states have enacted similar provisions. *See*, e.g., ALA. CODE tit. 15-13-62 (1975); MINN. STAT. ANN. tit. 19 Statute 53 (1964 Purdon) (suspended by PA. R. CRIM. P. Statute 4018); TENN. CODE ANN. Statute 40-1227 (1975); TEX. CODE CRIM. PROC. Art. 17.16 (Vernon 1977); UTAH CODE ANN. tit. 77-43-22 (1953). At least two states have modified the common law. *See* TEX. CODE CRIM. PROC. Art. 17-19 (Vernon 1977) (which requires an arrest warrant) and CAL. PENAL CODE Statute 847.5 (1970 West) (which requires extradition procedures in order to transport a fugitive principal back to the jurisdiction from which he escaped). *See* section III(D) *infra*.

59. 165 Neb. 503, 86 N.W. 2d 373 (1957) (proceeding on an application of a bail bondsman for discharge and exoneration of his bail bond where the state moved for forfeiture of the bond).

60. *Id.* at 507, 86 N.W. 2d at 377.

61. 50 Del. 497, 501, 135 A. 2d 137, 139 (1957) (writ of habeas corpus by a prisoner contending that he was improperly arrested by his bail bondsman in Pennsylvania and returned to Delaware without extradition proceedings).

62. *See* section II *supra*.

63. 250 F. Supp. 512 (D. Neb. 1965).

64. *Id.* at 513.

65. *Id.* at 513-514.

66. *Id.*

67. *Id.* This arrest was made in violation of CAL. PENAL CODE Statute 847.5 (West 1970). Apparently the defendant's agent was not arrested for violation of the statute and Judge Robinson made no mention of this violation. *See* note 58 *supra* and text accompanying notes 150-55 *infra*.

68. *Id.* at 514-15.

69. *Id.* at 515.

70. *Id.*

71. *Id.* Judge Robinson summarized the entire problem well, stating: "One purpose of allowing a person his liberty by use of a bond is to prevent such person from being imprisoned for an unnecessary length of time without the [c]ourt losing the assurance that such person will appear in court at the appointed time. The bondsman has a duty signified by his written contract to present his principal before the court. This is the basic reason for the rule which gives the bondsman the right to pursue and arrest his principal. Fundamental interests of justice and society require that a surety in a criminal case be given greater authority than the other types of sureties and bondsmen. But this authority is conditioned on the recognition of his duty to the court to present the principal before the court. If this fundamental condition is not obeyed, the entire purpose for which bonds are given and, collaterally, the rule vesting broad authority in the bondsman will be effectively thwarted. It is the finding of this [c]ourt that whenever a bondsman takes *undue* advantage of his justly granted and needed authority in violation of

his duty to the granting court and such *undue advantage results in injury or damage* to his principal or another party, that bondsman should and will be rendered liable for any damage caused as a result of an act or acts which would render liable any other person who was not vested with such authority." Id. (Emphasis added.)

Interestingly, while focusing on the tort liability of the defendant, Judge Robinson ignored the plaintiff's claim for violation of his civil rights. Presumably the required element of state action was missing. *See* section III(C) *infra*.

72. 250 F. Supp. at 515.

73. *See* section II *supra*.

74. 44 Ala. App. 171, 204 So. 2d 817 (1967). Though not actually a tort case, the elements of a trespass and an assault and battery were present.

75. *Id.* at 173, 204 So. 2d at 818.

76. *Id.* at 174, 204 So. 2d at 818-19.

77. *Id.* at 175, 204 So. 2d at 820.

78. *Id.* at 182, 204 So. 2d at 827.

79. *Id.* at 181, 204 So. 2d at 826.

80. *Id.*

81. *Id.* at 178-79, 204 So. 2d at 823.

82. *Id.* at 178, 204 So. at 823-24.

83. *Id.* 181, 204 So. 2d at 826. The judge also emphasized that the only legitimate purpose for such an arrest is to deliver the principal to the authorities, not to collect debts on bonds. *Id.* at 178, 204 So. 2d at 823-24.

As did the *McCaleb* Court, the court here determined that the bondsman had "reached beyond the mantle of protection afforded by the law to a bondsman." *McCaleb v. Peerless Ins. Co.*, 250 F. Supp. 512, 515 (D. Neb. 1965).

84. 51 Ala. App. 366, 285 So. 2d 923 (1973).

85. *Id.* at 368, 285 So. 2d at 924-25. The son had failed to appear at a court hearing on a drunk driving charge. *Id.* at 366, 285 So. 2d at 925.

86. *Id.* at 370, 285 So. 2d at 926-27. The court did not correctly construe this to be the law and therefore the verdict was reversed and the case remanded.

87. *Id.* at 368, 285 So. 2d at 925. The court stated: [t]here is a strong public policy in preventing the principal from "jumping bond" and because of this, the surety is permitted a large discretion as to the steps necessary to effect the apprehension of the principal.

88. 44 Ala. App. 171, 204 So. 2d 817 (1967). *See* text accompanying notes 74-83 *supra*.

89. 51 Ala. App. at 368, 285 So. 2d at 925. The court gave little attention to the possible or actual occurrences of abuses, except to say that those making arrests could use no more force than is reasonably necessary. *Id.* at 369, 285 So. 2d at 927. The court could have voiced support for stricter controls on bail bondsmen while still

holding that the defendant had not abused the powers traditionally granted bondsmen. In *Shine*, the court also acknowledged the need for these powers but did not allow those arguments to override the need for controls in view of the excesses of local bondsmen and their agents. 44 Ala. App. at 181, 204 So. 2d at 826.

90. 527 S.W. 2d 84 (Tenn. S. Ct. 1975).

91. *Id.* at 85.

92. *Id.* at 86.

83. *Id.*

94. *Id.* TENN. CODE ANN. Statute 40-1227 (1975).

95. 527 S.W. 2d at 89.

96. 42 U.S.C. Statutes 1983, 1985 (1970) and 18 U.S.C. Statute 242 (1970) have been employed in these cases, *See* notes 100, 112, and 122 *infra.*

97. 189 F. Supp. 559 (E.D. Ark. 1960).

98. *Id.* at 560.

99. *Id.* at 561.

100. 18 U.S.C. Statute 242 (1970) which provides: "Whoever, under color of any law, statute, ordinance, regulation, or custom, *willfully* subjects any inhabitant of any State, Territory, or District to the deprivation of any rights, privileges, or immunities secured or protected by the Constitution or laws of the United States, or to different punishments, pains, or penalties on account of such inhabitant being an alien or by reason of his color, or race, than are prescribed for the punishment of citizens, shall be fined not more than $1,000 or imprisoned not more than one year, or both; and if death results shall be subject to imprisonment for any term or for life." (Emphasis added.)

101. 189 F. Supp. at 565.

102. *Id.* at 564. The violation was of constitutional due process.

103. *Id.* at 564-65. *See* note 100 *supra.*

104. *Id.* at 565.

105. *Id.*

106. The court may have construed the statute too narrowly when it upbraided the defendant in harsh terms for his actions, while on the other hand deciding that his actions were not accompanied by any specific intent to deprive the fugitive of his constitutional rights. 189 S. Supp. at 564. It is certain that the defendant was ignorant of the statute and perhaps even of the Constitution, but ignorance of the law normally is not a valid defense. LaFAVE & SCOTT, CRIMINAL LAW 356 (1972). It is also certain that whatever Trunko did, he did willfully. To require a conscious willfulness to deprive a person of his constitutional rights is, in effect, to vitiate the statute and make convictions close to impossible. See *Screws v. United States*, 325 U.S. 91, 101-07 (1945), which discusses this question at length.

107. 189 F. Supp. at 565. The court also may have contradicted itself by damning the defendant for his *in terrorem* tactics while implying that if the defendant had identified himself properly, his actions would

have been beyond reproach. In other words, what is outrageous if done in the name of the law is acceptable if done by private persons. *See* note 100 and accompanying text *supra.*

108. 282 F. Supp. 571 (E.D. Tenn. 1968).

109. *Id.* at 572.

110. *Id.*

111. *Id.*

112. *Id.* at 572-73. The plaintiff sued under 42 U.S.C. Statute 1983 (1970), which provides: Every person who, under color of any statute, ordinance, regulation, custom, or usage, of any State or Territory, subjects, or causes to be subjected, any citizen of the United States or other person within the jurisdiction thereof to the deprivation of any rights, privileges, or immunities secured by the Constitution and laws, shall be liable to the party injured in an action at law, suit in equity, or other proper proceeding for redress.

113. 282 F. Supp. at 573.

114. *Id.* at 573.

115. *Id.* at 572.

116. *Id.*

117. *See* section III(B) *supra.*

118. 282 F. Supp. at 572-73.

119. 299 F. Supp. 429 (D. Minn. 1969).

120. *Id.* at 431.

121. *Id.* at 432.

122. *Id.* at 431. Curtis sued under 42 U.S.C. Statutes 1983 and 1985 (1970). For the text of section 1983, *see* note 112 *supra.* Section 1985 provides for a civil cause of action against two or more persons who

123. 299 F. Supp. at 434.

124. *Id.* at 435.

125. *Id.* at 435. Curiously, the court did not address the plaintiff's tort claim for false imprisonment. The court in *McCaleb v. Peerless Ins. Co.*, 250 F. Supp. 512 (D. Neb. 1965) (*see* text accompanying notes 63-72 *supra*) did the opposite, ignoring the civil rights claim of the plaintiff and holding for the plaintiff solely on the basis of his tort claim. In *Curtis*, the court could have found in the plaintiff's favor despite his lack of civil rights action, if the arrest and imprisonment had been otherwise tortious. Clearly, in view of the facts and the prevailing law, it was not.

126. 299 F. Supp. at 435.

127. *Id.* at 433, 435.

128. 333 F. Supp. 35 (E.D. Pa. 1971).

129. *Id.* at 36-37, 39.

130. *Id.* at 37-38. Pa. Stat. Ann. tit 19 Statute 53 (1964 Purdon, suspended Supp. 1977-78).

131. 333 F. Supp. at 37. The suit was brought under 42 U.S.C. Statutes 1983 and 1985 (1970). *See* notes 100, 122 *supra.*

132. 333 F. Supp. at 38-39.

133. *Id.* at 39.

134. *Id.* The court also held that there was no conspiracy in violation of 42 U.S.C. Statute 1985 (1970). Although his action was under color of state law, the court clerk was also exonerated because under statute 1983, state judicial and quasi-judicial officers are immune from suit. *Id.* at 38-39.

135. *Curtis v. Peerless Ins. Co.* 299 F. Supp. 429 (D. Minn. 1969); *Thomas v. Miller*, 282 F. Supp. 571 (E.D. Tenn. 1968).

136. *See* note 58 *supra.*

137. If the activities of bail bondsmen were to be considered state action, requirements of due process would apply to those actions. Failure to meet those requirements would then make recovery under the Civil Rights Acts likely. Actual physical abuse, essential to any tort recovery, would not be necessary although if it did occur there would be grounds for both civil rights and tort liability. At any rate, extension of state action to cover bail bondsmen would go far toward reducing abuses.

138. *See* note 46 and accompanying text *supra.*

139. *See* note 58 *supra.*

140. 7 Johns. (N.Y.) 145 (1810).

141. 4 Conn. 166 (1822).

142. *Poteete v. Olive*, 527 S.W. 2d 84 (Tenn. S. Ct. 1975).

143. 541 S.W. 2d 162 (Tex. Cr. App. 1976).

144. *Id.* at 163.

145. *Id.*

146. *Id.*

147. TEX. CODE CRIM. PROC. Art 17.19 (Vernon 1977).

148. 541 S.W. 2d at 164. Again, the defendant was convicted for failure to comply with procedures rather than for the violent tactics used to make the arrest. The court should have addressed the problem of such violence, but it rejected the invitation to reinforce *Shine v. State*, 44 Ala. App. 171, 204 So. 2d 817 (1967), just as the Tennessee court did in *Poteete v. Olive*, 527 S.W. 2d 84 (Tenn. S. Ct. 1975). *See* notes 74-83 and 90-95 and accompanying text *supra.*

149. As noted above, arrests made with a certified copy of the bond are not usually held to be under color of state law. *See* section III(C) *supra.*

150. CAL. PENAL CODE Statute 847.5 (West 1970).

151. *Id.*

152. *Id.* Pending the hearing the suspect may be admitted to local bail.

153. *Id.*

154. *Id.*

155. *See* note, *Bailbondsmen and the Fugitive Accused—The Need for Formal Removal Procedures*, 73 Yale L.J. 1098 (1964) dealing extensively with the need for extradition procedures in this area and advocating nationwide enactment of statutes such as that in California.

156. U.S. CONST., amends V and XIV.

APPENDIX C

Liability of Bail Bondsmen under Section 1983

Washington and Lee Law Review
Volume 42, Number 1

Various forms of bail[1] release currently exist in the United States.[2] In one form of bail release, the court requires the accused to contract with an individual or agency in the business of writing bonds.[3] If the professional bondsman writes and posts the bonds with the court,[4] the bondsman becomes a surety on the contract.[5] The surety is liable to the court setting the bail for the full face value of the bond should the accused, or principal, not appear.[6] However, courts generally will provide the surety with a specified period of time in which to find and return the fugitive principal to the court's jurisdiction to avoid forfeiture on the bond.[7] Ironically, the law provides greater authority to a bail bondsman in returning a fugitive principal who has violated the conditions of bail, than the law provides to a law enforcement officer returning an escaped prisoner.[8]

The prevailing view in most courts today is that bondsmen possess extremely broad common-law grants of authority in effectuating the arrest of a principal.[9] The United States Supreme Court first addressed the issue of the authority of bondsmen in 1869 in *Reese v. United*

States.[10] In *Reese*, the sureties had posted a bond for a principal charged with land fraud.[11] Without informing the sureties, the government gave the principal permission to leave the United States.[12] When the principal failed to appear at subsequent trial dates, the United States Circuit Court for the District of California ordered a forfeiture on the bond.[13] The United States Supreme Court reversed, holding that the precise terms of the contract between the surety and the principal limited the liability of the surety.[14] In reaching its decision, the *Reese* Court addressed the issue of the common-law authority of sureties.[15] The Court stated that a principal is subject to the complete custody of the surety to the extent that the surety at any time may arrest and surrender the principal to the court issuing the bond.[16] Additionally, the *Reese* Court stated that the surety may exercise the arrest power only within the territory of the United States.[17]

In 1872, the Supreme Court issued the seminal statement concerning the common-law powers of sureties in *Taylor v. Taintor.*[18] The issue in *Taylor*, as in *Reese*, concerned a forfeiture of a bond.[19] In *Taylor*, the bondsmen had posted an 8,000 dollar bond in Connecticut for a principal who faced a charge of grand larceny.[20] Before the principal could appear at trial, however, the Governor of Maine requested the arrest of the principal on a Maine burglary charge.[21] At the time of the principal's Connecticut trial for grand larceny, the principal was imprisoned legally in Maine.[22] The sureties sued to recover the amount of the bond claiming impossibility of performance of the contract.[23] The Supreme Court held that since the sureties' dominion over the principal was so complete, the sureties were under obligation to keep the principal within the sureties' jurisdiction.[24] The sureties, therefore, had to forfeit the bond.[25] The *Taylor* Court reaffirmed the almost unlimited authority and discretion of sureties to arrest and deliver a principal to the court issuing the bond.[26]

The next major case addressing the issue of a surety's

power over a principal was *Fitzpatrick v. Williams.*[27] In *Fitzpatrick*, the New Orleans police arrested Fitzpatrick on affidavits charging the accused with having committed an offense in the state of Washington, and with being a fugitive from justice.[28] Despite dismissal of the charges, Fitzpatrick remained in the custody of the New Orleans police.[29] Fitzpatrick applied for a writ of habeas corpus.[30] A bonding company intervened in the proceedings, alleging that the company had posted a 1,500 dollar bond.[31] The bonding company asked the court to order the sheriff to surrender Fitzpatrick to the company's agent.[32] The trial court denied Fitzpatrick's writ and ordered the sheriff to surrender Fitzpatrick to the agent.[33] The United States Court of Appeals for the Fifth Circuit affirmed the denial of the writ on the basis of the broad arrest powers granted to sureties.[34] While reaffirming the *Taylor* common-law principles, however, the *Fitzpatrick* court emphasized a slightly different rationale for granting broad arrest powers to sureties.[35] In the *Fitzpatrick* decision, the Fifth Circuit stressed the private contract aspect of the surety-principal relationship.[36] The Fifth Circuit stated that the authority of a surety to recapture a principal is not a matter of criminal procedure, but instead arises from a private contract between a surety and a principal.[37] Because the right of recapture is a private right involving no governmental procedure, the *Fitzpatrick* court concluded that a surety has no need to obtain an arrest warrant or to seek extradition when returning a principal across states lines.[38] The lower courts have upheld the basic common-law principles enunciated in *Reese*, *Taylor* and *Fitzpatrick* on numerous occasions.[39]

The bondsman's source of authority to arrest and surrender the principal derives not only from the common law, but also from state statutes.[40] Several states have eliminated commercial bail as a method of pretrial release.[41] Some states have attempted to modify the common law concerning bail bondsmen by regulating surety arrest conduct.[42] In other states, however, courts view the relevant statute as merely codifying the common law, and determine the scope of the surety's authority by the principles described in *Taylor*.[43] Almost all states that permit the activities of professional bondsmen have failed to enact statutes which establish procedural safeguards controlling surety arrests.[44]

The lack of procedural safeguards in surety arrests has resulted in many cases of surety abuse of principals[45] and their families.[46] Because sureties possess such universally accepted authority to make arrests, courts may prefer to dispose of particular instances of surety abuse of principals by relying on tenuous analysis rather than impose liability on a surety for abusing his authority.[47] For example, in *McCaleb v. Peerless Insurance Co.*,[48] the principal, McCaleb, instituted suit to recover damages in tort for false arrest and imprisonment, illegal detention, violation of civil liberties.[49] McCaleb, who had violated certain traffic laws in Omaha, contracted with defendant Vinci, a bondsman for Peerless Insurance Company, to post a 200 dollar bond.[50] McCaleb left Omaha for California and did not return for the scheduled court appearance.[51] Vinci went to California and hired another agent who arrested McCaleb at his parents' home and took McCaleb to the local jail.[52] After Vinci gained control of McCaleb's car, Vinci took McCaleb out of jail and drove McCaleb around the state for eighty hours.[53] Vinci placed McCaleb in different jails throughout California during the 80 hour trip.[54] Vinci shackled McCaleb around the waist and wrists and kept the shackles on at all times that McCaleb was not in jail.[55] Vinci and McCaleb reached Omaha five days after the initial arrest.[56] Upon arriving in Omaha, Vinci took the title to McCaleb's automobile and forced McCaleb to sign a release.[57] Thereupon, Vinci told McCaleb to leave Nebraska, although McCaleb was scheduled to appear before the municipal court of the city of Omaha in one hour.[58] Vinci never did surrender McCaleb to the Omaha municipal court.[59] *McCaleb*, a 1965 decision, is the first reported case in which a court held a bondsman, who had exceeded his authority as surety, liable to the principal in tort.[60] Despite the abuse of the principal by the surety, the *McCaleb* court awarded monetary damages to the principal on the grounds that the bondsmen had not arrested McCaleb for the purpose of surrendering McCaleb to the proper authorities.[61] The decision in *McCaleb* does not indicate whether the Nebraska court would have imposed tort liability on the surety if the surety had surrendered McCaleb to the court.

Recently, litigants have challenged the practices and authority of bondsmen under section 1983 of Title 42 of the United States Code.[62] Section 1983 provides a remedy for deprivation of rights secured by the Constitution and laws of the United States when the deprivation takes place "under color of state law."[63] To prevail against a surety in a section 1983 suit, a principal must show that a bondsman acted under color of state law.[64] Additionally, a principal must show that the action of the bondsman deprived the principal of a constitutional or legal right.[65]

To date, four courts have held that bondsmen were acting under color of state law in arresting a principal.[66] In *United States v. Trunko*,[67] a bondsman holding a commission as a special deputy sheriff displayed a badge and a court-issued bench warrant when arresting the principal.[68] The United States District Court for the Eastern District of Ohio held that because the bondsman possessed apparent authority of the state, the bondsman acted under color of state law.[69] In *Smith v. Rosenbaum*,[70] the United States District Court for the Eastern District of Pennsylvania held that the act of lodging a bail piece[71] against a principal pursuant to the Pennsylvania law constituted an act under color of state law.[72] Similarly, in *Maynard v. Kear*,[73] the agents of a bonding company purported to act pursuant to a Virginia state bench warrant in arresting the principal in Ohio.[74] Consequently, the United States District Court for the Northern District of Ohio held that the bondsmen were acting under color of state law.[75] The *Maynard* court reasoned that the State of Virginia had lent authority to the private bondsmen when the bondsmen arrested the principal in Ohio pursuant to a bench warrant obtained under a Virginia state statute.[76] Finally, in *Hill v. Toll*,[77] the United States District court for the Eastern District of Pennsylvania also held that a bondsman, acting pursuant to a state statute that accorded bondsmen the right to conduct their business affairs by use of physical coercion,[78] was acting under color of state law.[79] Other courts, however, have refused to impose liability pursuant to section 1983 on bail bondsmen, determining that the bondsmen were not acting under color of state law.[80]

Presently, three courts have addressed the issue of which specific constitutional rights are applicable to the surety arrest procedure to meet the constitional deprivation requirement in section 1983 actions.[81] In *Hill v. Toll*,[82] the principal attacked the validity of his arrest as a breach of state contract law.[83] The United States District Court for the Eastern District of Pennsylvania held that because the principal had not alleged that the arrest was unconstitutional, the single allegation of breach of contract law could not form the basis for relief under section 1983.[84] The *Hill* court held, however, that the beating and robbery allegations of the principal constituted a claim cognizable under section 1983.[85] The court reasoned that allegations of beating and robbery qualified as a claim of an unreasonable search and seizure and, therefore, constituted a violation of the principal's fourth and fourteenth amendment rights.[86] One year after *Hill*, the United States District Court for the Eastern District of Pennsylvania faced a similar breach of contract argument in *Smith v. Rosenbaum*.[87] In *Rosenbaum*, the principal argued that the sureties had breached the bail contract by lodging bail pieces against the principal, thereby depriving the principal of liberty without due process of law.[88] The *Rosenbaum* court stated that the sureties had not deprived the principal of liberty without due process by revoking the bail bond contract because recent actions of the principal justified the revocation.[89] Consequently, the *Rosenbaum* court held that the principal had failed to prove that the sureties had violated any of the principal's rights secured under the Constitution.[90] Finally, in *Maynard v. Kear*,[91] the United States District Court for the Northern District of Ohio addressed the possible constitutional claims of the principal, under the fourth, sixth and eighth amendments in the principal's section 1983 action against the surety.[92] The *Maynard* court focused on the right of a principal to be free from the use of unreasonable means and force in a surety arrest as the most relevant and applicable fourth amendment right actionable under section 1983.[93] Additionally, the *Maynard* court stated that for the eighth amendment protections to extend to surety arrests, the alleged mistreatment must rise to the constitutional dimensions of cruel and unusual punishment.[94] Finally the *Maynard* court concluded that the principal had no claim under the sixth amendment of a violation by the bondsman of a principal's right to extradition proceedings.[95] The *Maynard* court noted that under the common law a recapture of the principal by a bondsman required no extradition proceedings.[96]

The United States Supreme Court's recent decision in *Lugar v. Edmondson Oil Co.*[97] clarifies the threshold requirements that a constitutionally deprived individual such as an abused principal must establish when bringing a section 1983 suit premised upon the fourteenth amendment.[98] The fourteenth amendment to the United States Constitution provides that no state may deprive any person of life, liberty or property without due process of law.[99] Because the fourteenth amendment applies to the states, only conduct that a court may fairly characterize as state action, and not as private action, will constitute a violation of the amendment.[100] Section 1983 requires both a deprivation of a right secured by the Constitution or the laws of the United States, and that the deprivation result from an act under color of state law.[101] In *Lugar*, the Court addressed the relationship between the section 1983 requirement of action under color of state law and the fourteenth amendment requirement of state action.[102] The *Lugar* Court held that whenever state action is present, then action under color of state law is present for purposes of a suit under section 1983.[103] Consequently, in a section 1983 suit involving the fourteenth amendment, a trial court will limit its inquiry to the state action issue.[104]

The *Lugar* Court established a two-step procedure for determining whether state action is present.[105] First, the exercise of some right or privilege that the state has created, or the exercise of a state imposed rule of conduct, must cause the deprivation of the constitutional right.[106] Second, the party charged with the deprivation must be a person who the courts fairly may characterize as a "state actor."[107] The two steps merge when the accused individual is a state official, but a court must treat the two steps separately when the constitutional claim is against a private party.[108] When a section 1983 suit is directed against a private party, four tests apply in determining whether that private party is a state actor.[109] The *Lugar* Court declined to hold whether the tests identifying a state actor operate separately or as a whole.[110] In the first test, the "public function" test, a court considers whether the private party performs that [which] traditionally is within the exclusive prerogative of the state.[111] Under the second test, the "state compulsion" test, the state is responsible for a private decision only when the state has exercised coercive power or has provided significant encouragement, either covert or overt, to such an extent that the private decision becomes a state decision.[112] The "nexus" test, the third test, concerns the question of whether the state has reached a position of interdependence with the challenged activities of an otherwise private individual so as to make the state a joint participant in the challenged activity.[113] The fourth test applicable to the state actor issue, the "joint action" test, concerns whether the private party has participated jointly with state officials in a prohibited act sufficiently to characterize that party as a state actor.[114] In *Lugar*, the Court held that a private party's joint participation with state officials under a procedurally defective statute in the seizure of disputed property was sufficient to characterize that party as a state actor for purposes of the fourteenth amendment.[115] To meet the first step in the requirement for determining the presence of state action, the Court held that the statutory scheme permitting the unconstitutional attachment of property upon the *ex parte* application of one party to a private dispute was a product of state action.[116] Consequently, the plaintiff had presented a valid cause of action under section 1983 by challenging the state statute as procedurally defective under the due process clause.[117]

In light of the *Lugar* opinion, a principal must establish two elements to meet the state action, or color of state law requirement. First, a principal must demonstrate that the surety's conduct resulted from the exercise of a right or privilege which the state had created in a state statute.[118] Courts essentially have met this step by holding that state action occurs when a surety acts pursuant to a state statute authorizing surety arrests under a bench warrant or bail piece.[119] Alternatively, a principal may demonstrate that the surety's conduct resulted from a right exercised under a procedurally defective statute.[120] A statute is procedurally defective either because the statute has failed to establish appropriate safeguards governing surety arrests,[121] or permits the attachment of property upon the *ex parte* application of one party to a private dispute.[122] To meet the second element of the state action requirement, the principal must demonstrate that the surety is a "state actor" by applying one or more of the tests discussed in *Lugar*.[123] Under the public function test, a court may perceive the bondsman as exercising the power of arrest, the exercise of which constitutes a traditionally exclusive function of the state.[124] Under the state compulsion test, a court may conclude that the bondsman is a state actor when the bondsman acts pursuant to a state statute authorizing an arrest warrant or bail piece as the basis for the bondsman's authority to arrest.[125] A court may conclude under the nexus test that a sufficient symbiotic relationship exists between a state and the activities of a bondsman to make the bondsman a state actor.[126] A symbiotic relationship results from the state's regulation of, benefit from, and conferral of the arrest power on sureties.[127] Finally, a court may conclude under the joint activity test that the surety has been a joint participant with state officials in arresting a principal. A surety acts jointly with state officials when the surety obtains bail pieces and bench warrants.[128] A surety also acts jointly with state officials when the surety obtains a principal's release from jail or uses jail facilities while returning a principal to the jurisdiction of the court issuing the bond.[129] Additionally, a surety acts jointly with state officials when state law enforcement officers aid a surety in arresting a principal.[130] By demonstrating that a surety is a state actor and that the surety's conduct has resulted from a right or privilege which the state has created, a principal will have met the state action or color of state law requirement necessary to bring suit under section 1983.[131]

After meeting the color of state law requirement under section 1983, a principal must demonstrate that the actions of a surety have deprived the principal of a right secured under the United States Constitution.[132] The principal must claim that the state has deprived the principal of liberty or property without due process of law conferred under the fourteenth amendment.[133] By means of the due process clause, the fourteenth amendment selectively incorporates certain provisions of the Bill of Rights.[134] Generally, the Supreme Court will incorporate under the fourteenth amendment a right that the Court considers fundamental to the American scheme of justice.[135] The Supreme Court has held that the fourth amendment protections against unreasonable searches and seizures and the requirements for obtaining search warrants are among the fundamental rights which the fourteenth amendment protects.[136] A principal, therefore, may assert fourth amendment rights in a section 1983 suit as violations of the fourteenth amendment due process clause.

Prior case law has not addressed specifically the bounds of fourth amendment rights in the context of a rearrest by a bondsman.[137] The fourth amendment to the United States Constitution protects the right of the people to be secure in their persons, houses, papers, and effects, against unreasonable searches and seizures.[138] By means of fourteenth amendment incorporation, the fourth amendment also requires that the state issue warrants only upon probable cause, naming the specific places to be searched and the persons or things to be seized.[139] Upon establishment of a surety's conduct as state action, certain areas of fourth amendment protections such as the requirements of the use of reasonable force and means,[140] warrants,[141] and hearings[142] are applicable to the surety arrest.[143]

Under the fourth amendment, arrests by police officers may not involve more than the use of reasonable or necessary force.[144] Reasonable force is that force necessary under the circumstances to make the arrest or prevent the escape of the accused.[145] The United States District

Court for the District of Minnesota has noted that sureties must stay within the bounds of reasonable means, including force, in arresting principals, and has implied that sureties would be liable in tort to principals for improper custody.[146] The Alabama Court of Appeals has indicated that courts should control the use of unnecessary force by sureties by controlling the use of weapons.[147] According to the Alabama Court of Appeals, courts should investigate every occasion in which a surety claims to need weapons and should require law enforcement officials to accompany the surety on such occasions.[148] Furthermore, arrests by police officers for misdemeanors when the arrestee's resistance is nonviolent will not justify the use of weapons.[149] As a general rule, in the case of a misdemeanor, an officer has no right, except in self-defense, to shoot or kill the offender in effecting the arrest, even when the offender flees.[150] Since many of the violent arrests in which bondsmen use weapons occur in cases of misdemeanors and involve small amounts of money,[151] a court may wish to extend the misdemeanor principle to surety arrests.

In addition to the requirement of reasonable force, courts have interpreted the fourth amendment to require an arresting officer to give notice of the officer's identity and purpose when demanding entrance into a dwelling place.[152] The prevailing view is that entry without notice is possible only when the officer acts on a reasonable good-faith belief that compliance with the notice requirement would frustrate an arrest, endanger lives, or permit the destruction of evidence.[153] In *Read v. Case*,[154] the Connecticut Supreme Court held that a bondsman in a surety arrest must notify a principal of the reason for the bondsman's appearance and must request admission before making any attempt to enter the principal's home forcibly.[155] The *Read* Court noted that the only valid excuse for a bondsman's failure to meet the demand-notice requirement was the bondsman's belief that his personal safety or that of an agent was in jeopardy from the intended violence of a principal.[156] Requiring sureties to identify themselves and to give notice of their legal power and the reason for the arrest would benefit principals since recapture situations often involve agents, commonly called "bounty hunters" whom principals never have seen,[157] and who do not indicate the reasons for the arrest.[158]

In addition to requirements of reasonable force and means, the fourth amendment imposes certain warrant requirements on police officers.[159] Although the Supreme Court has expressed a strong preference that police officers should obtain arrest warrants when practicable, the Court has not required the use of arrest warrants in all circumstances.[160] Relying on a strong common-law tradition, the Supreme Court has held that warrantless public arrests are permissible if based on probable cause.[161] In *Payton v. New York*,[162] the United States Supreme Court addressed the issue of whether the Constitution requires a police officer to obtain a warrant to enter private premises to make an arrest.[163] Confirming that the fourth amendment draws a firm line at the entrance of a house for the seizure of either persons or property, the Supreme Court held that a warrant is necessary to cross the threshold of a home to make a routine felony arrest of a fugitive, absent exigent circumstances.[164] The Constitution also requires a police officer to obtain a search warrant before entering the house of a third party, absent exigent circumstances, to arrest a fugitive.[165]

In considering the issue of whether a surety must obtain an arrest warrant for a public arrest of a principal, courts have relied on the common-law tradition of *Taylor*[166] and *Fitzpatrick*[167] to hold that a surety does not need a warrant.[168] Even the *Maynard* court, the only court to consider in depth the fourth amendment rights of principals under the Constitution, was hesitant to require arrest warrants.[169] In *United States v. Holmes*,[170] however, the United States Court of Appeals for the Seventh Circuit addressed the issue of whether a warrantless rearrest by federal officers of a bailed defendant was valid.[171] While recognizing that law enforcement officers may rearrest principals for a variety of reasons, the Seventh Circuit concluded that the fourth amendment applied to the rearrest of a bailed defendant by federal officers.[172] The *Holmes* court emphasized that the fourth amendment requires both a reasonable foundation for a criminal charge and the avoidance of arbitrary and unreasonable interferences with privacy.[173] A court could apply the Seventh Circuit's reasoning in *Holmes* to a surety arrest situation, and conclude that warrants for public arrests by sureties are necessary.[174]

Similarly, a court may wish to impose a warrant requirement before permitting a bondsman to enter a principal's home or the home of a third party.[175] The *Taylor* court specified that, if necessary, a bondsman may break and enter a principal's house to make an arrest, but *Taylor* neither supports nor prohibits the proposition that a surety may enter the dwelling of a third party.[176] However, entry into a third-party dwelling was at issue in the case of *Livingston v. Browder*.[177] In *Livingston*, a mother brought suit against a bondsman who had entered the mother's house without permission and arrested her son.[178] The *Livingston* court held that a surety has the authority to enter the dwelling of a third party to arrest the principal.[179] The *Livingston* court, however, imposed certain conditions on sureties entering third-party dwellings.[180] The *Livingston* court stated that the surety must have reasonable and just cause to believe the principal is in the dwelling, must properly identify himself, and must use reasonable means to gain entry.[181] Relying on the rationale expressed in *Livingston* and on the policies supported by the United States Supreme Court in recent decisions requiring police officers to obtain arrest and search warrants, a court reasonably could impose a warrant requirement on sureties acting under color of state law before allowing entry into homes or private dwellings.[182]

In addition to requiring the use of reasonable force and means, and the use of warrants in appropriate circumstances, the fourth and fourteenth amendments also require hearings in certain situations before a state may deprive an individual of liberty or property.[183] In examining violations of a principal's constitutional rights in a section 1983 suit, courts may compare the principal's right to a hearing to that right which is available to an arrestee.[184] Additionally, a court may compare the principal's right to a hearing to that of a probationer or parolee in the correctional process prior to revocation of probation or parole.[185] Finally, a court may compare the principal's right to a hearing to the right established for state enforcement of a private contract right.[186]

The United States Supreme Court has addressed the issue of an arrestee's right to a hearing during the arrest procedure. Under guidelines established by the Supreme Court, since an arresting officer may arrest without a warrant, the Constitution does not require a hearing to determine probable cause prior to an arrest.[187] Following the arrest, however, the fourth amendment requires a judicial determination of probable cause as a prerequisite to extended restraint on liberty.[188] In such a hearing, the fourth amendment does not require the full panoply of constitutional safeguards associated with an adversarial hearing.[189] Instead, the hearing may be an informal procedure before a judicial officer who is to make a determination of probable cause for detention using the same standard of probable cause as that required for an arrest.[190] If a hearing is not conducted prior to the arrest, the judicial officer must make the determination of probable cause promptly after the arrest.[191]

If a court determines that a bondsman has acted under

color of state law and considers the bondsman's actions to be analogous to those of an officer rearresting an individual on bail, then the court may find that a hearing is necessary at some point in the surety-arrest procedure.[192] The purpose of the hearing would be to articulate the cause for the rearrest and to verify the identity of the arrestee.[193] Given the contractual nature of the bond agreement, valid causes for a rearrest would include breaking the bail contract by leaving the jurisdiction determined in the bail agreement, increased risk to the bondsman, or the simple desire of the bondsman to be relieved of the contractual obligation.[194] The United States Supreme Court has stated that an arrest hearing, whether held before or after an arrest, should furnish meaningful protection from unfounded interference with an arrestee's liberty.[195] A court could provide meaningful protection against interference with a principal's liberty by requiring a surety to promptly present the principal to a judicial officer in the jurisdiction in which the arrest takes place.[196] Prompt presentation balances the rightful power of the surety to revoke the contract with the due process requirements of protection of the rearrested individual under the fourth and fourteenth amendments.

A court also may analogize the right of a principal to a hearing upon revocation of the bail bond to the right of a parolee or a probationer to a hearing on revocation of parole or probation.[197] Under the due process clause of the fourteenth amendment, a parolee has a right to a reasonably prompt informal hearing, conducted by an impartial hearing officer near the place of the alleged parole violation, to determine if reasonable grounds exist to believe that the arrested parolee violated a parole condition.[198] A probationer also is entitled to a preliminary and final probation revocation hearing under the same conditions specified for a parolee.[199] Since parole and probation revocation are not part of the criminal prosecution, neither parolees nor probationers are entitled to a hearing subject to the full panoply of rights applicable to the criminal prosecution process.[200] For both parolees and probationers, however, the loss of significant liberty interests is involved in revocation of freedom, and due process mandates a hearing of some type.[201] If a court chooses to compare the revocation of parole and probation to the revocation of a bail bond, the issue of whether procedural protections demand a hearing for a principal will turn on the extent to which the principal will suffer a grievous loss and whether the nature of this loss is within the contemplation of the "liberty or property" language of the fourteenth amendment.[202] Since a principal, like a parolee, suffers a loss of a significant liberty interest, a court could analogize the revocation of bail to the revocation of parole and probation, and impose a due process requirement of a hearing before the revocation of bail.[203]

If a court did analogize the hearing requirements for revocation of parole to the bail situation, the differences between principals and parolees indicate that the hearings would serve different functions.[204] Implicit in the system of parole is the idea that the parolee is entitled to retain his liberty so long as the parolee abides by the conditions of the parole.[205] Implicit in the bail bond system is the right of the surety to revoke the bond for any reason the surety chooses.[206] The purpose of a parole hearing is to determine whether the parolee did, in fact, violate the conditions of parole and whether revocation of parole is the best solution.[207] In contrast to a parole revocation hearing, a hearing for a principal may occur before or after the arrest and should reflect both the interests of the bondsman on the contract as well as the interests of the state in assuring that a bondsman arrests pursuant to a valid contract and that the bondsman arrests the individual named in the contract.[208]

A court could also analogize the issue of whether due process requires a hearing for principals arrested by sureties acting under color of state law to cases concerning state deprivation of property.[209] According to traditional case law, the contract between the surety and the principal is a private contract and not a matter of criminal procedure.[210] Inserted into a typical bond contract is a clause authorizing the surety to arrest and surrender the principal at any time to the court issuing the bond.[211] Courts have continued to hold that the bonding contract is legal,[212] and, because the contract is private, some courts hold that the fourteenth amendment is not applicable to sureties exercising the arrest power.[213] When the surety is acting under color of state law, however, the analysis changes, because the state and the private party are enforcing a private contract right.[214] The issue then becomes whether due process rights, which apply to state deprivation of property interests under a bail bond contract, require notice and opportunity for a principal to be heard concurrent with the enforcement of specific provisions of the bail contract on the application of a surety.[215]

A leading United States Supreme Court case providing guidelines concerning the procedural due process required before a state can deprive an individual of a property interest pursuant to a private contract is *Fuentes v. Shevin*.[216] In *Fuentes*, the Court addressed the problem of replevin of goods purchased under an installment sales contract upon application of a private party.[217] The Pennsylvania and Florida statutes in question permitted a private party, without a hearing or prior notice to the other party, to obtain a prejudgment writ of replevin through a summary process of *ex parte* application to a court clerk.[218] The statutes required the sheriff to execute the writ by seizing the property.[219] The *Fuentes* Court held that the replevin provision of the state statutes were invalid under the fourteenth amendment since the provision constituted a deprivation of property without due process of law by denying the right of one party to the dispute an opportunity to be heard before the other party takes the chattels.[220] Additionally, the *Fuentes* court held that procedural due process requires an opportunity for a hearing before the state authorizes its agents to seize property in the possession of one person under the application of another.[221]

The *Fuentes* analysis arguably applies to the bail bond contract.[222] Under the bail bond contract, the liberty interest of a principal is at least as important to the principal as a property interest.[223] Since the right to be heard, whether liberty or property is at stake, is fundamental to the fourteenth amendment,[224] the right to be heard before rearrest under a bail bond contract is as constitutionally necessary as the right to be heard before replevin under an installment sales contract.[225] By analogy to *Fuentes*, therefore, a state court reasonably could mandate that a principal be accorded an opportunity for a hearing before a state authorizes bondsmen to seize the liberty interests of a principal in the principal's possession under the contract.[226]

The broad grant of authority to bail bondsmen by the courts[227] and by state statutes[228] has created a situation in which a surety may cause a principal to suffer a deprivation of rights.[229] To remedy this deprivation of rights, a principal may sue the bondsman under section 1983 of title 42 of the United States Code.[230] To prevail in an action under section 1983, the principal must prove that the bondsman acted under color of state law and that the bondsman deprived the principal of a right, privilege, or immunity secured under the constitution.[231] Under the *Lugar* analysis, a principal will present a valid cause of action under section 1983 if the principal challenges the state statute permitting surety arrests as procedurally defective under the due process clause of the fourteenth amendment.[232] Under the more traditional approach, a principal will present a valid cause of action under section 1983 by demonstrating state action[233] and a deprivation of a right under the fourteenth and fourth amendments.[234] Effective use of section 1983 will improve the quality of justice in the commercial bail bond system.

Mary Lee Doane

ENDNOTES

1. *See* Hatchett, *Filling In The Gaps of Virginia Bail Reform*, 14 U. Rich. L. Rev. 483, 484 (1980) (discussion of bail reform movement in Virginia). Under common law the term "bail" means release secured by surety. *Id.* Recent usage of the term "bail" has expanded the definition to include any release from custody regardless of the conditions imposed. *Id. See generally* State v. Mitchell, 59 Del. 11, ____, 212 A.2d 873, 874-84 (Del. Super. Ct. 1965) (discussion of history of bail). Bail originated in medieval England as a device to free untried prisoners. *Id.* at ____, 212 A.2d at 880. In this early period, a sheriff would release a prisoner on the promise of either the prisoner or a third party that the prisoner would appear for trial. *Id.* If the prisoner failed to return for trial, the third-party surety had to take the prisoner's place. *Id.* Consequently, to protect the surety's risk, the sheriff gave the surety custodial powers over the prisoner. *Id.* In time, the bail system evolved to permit sureties to forfeit money, instead of themselves, when the principal did not appear. *Id.* Eventually, the state transferred bailing functions from the sheriff's office to the justice of the peace. *Id.; see* Note, *Bail: An Ancient Practice Reexamined*, 70 Yale L.J. 966, 966-69 (1961) (discussion of history of bail).

2. *See* Toborg, *Bail Bondsmen and Criminal Courts*, 8 Just. Sys. J. 141, 142-43 (1983) (discussion of symbiotic relationship between bondsmen and criminal courts, and way in which bondsmen facilitate court operations). In determining bail, a trial judge has the authority to invoke one of four general forms of bail release. *Id.* at 141. First, the judge may release the accused on the condition that the accused promise to appear for subsequent court dates. *Id.* Second, the judge may release the accused to the custody of a pretrial release program, other agency, or a third party. *Id.* Third, the judge may require the accused to post a percentage of the amount of the bond, usually ten percent, with the court. *Id.* Courts using the third alternative generally refund most of the ten percent fee to a defendant who has appeared on the specified trial dates. *Id.* Finally, if a deposit bond is not feasible for the accused, the accused may contract with a professional bondsman. *Id.*

3. *See id.* at 141. The accused pays the bondsman a fee, typically ten percent of the amount of the bond, in return for writing the bond. *Id.* at 142.

4. *See id.* at 142. The bondsman has total discretion in deciding whether to write the bond. *Id.* The bondsman will base his decision

on financial considerations and the expected ease or difficulty of producing the defendant. *Id.; see also* Reiss, *The Long Arm of John Light's Law*, 4 Wash. Post. Mag., Jan. 29, 1984 (description of Washington, D.C. bail bond business from bondsman's perspective) [hereinafter cited as *The Long Arm*]. In Washington, D.C., the complicated process of writing and posting a bond may take hours. *Id.* at 11. The jailed defendant or the defendant's lawyer calls the family who then calls a bondsman. *Id.* A family member then visits the bondsman and fills out the bond application. *Id.* Next, the bondsman investigates the family member's identification as well as the charge sheet and the bail agency's sheet, both of which describe the prior arrest record of the accused. *Id.* At this point, the bondsman decides whether to write the bond by assessing the risks involved. *Id.* Generally the bondsman writes bonds for 25 out of 100 applicants. *Id.* After deciding to write the bond, the bondsman fills out a bond sheet and a jail release sheet, and deposits the papers in the superior court finance office. *Id.* The finance office calls the jail, and the jail verifies the charges and the amount of the bond. *Id.* The bondsman then picks up the accused at the receiving and discharge area of the jail, escorts the accused to the finance office, and signs the bond swearing to abide by the rules and conditions that the judge has set. *Id.* As compensation, the bondsman receives ten percent of the bond. *Id.* A judge usually will give the bondsman fourteen days to catch a bail jumper, but if the police capture the jumper first, the bondsman probably will forfeit the bond money. *Id.* at 12.

5. *See* Toborg, *supra* note 2, at 142; *see also* State v. Mitchell, 59 Del. 11, ______, 212 A.2d 873, 884 (Del. Super. Ct. 1965) (description of bail bond as contract between government on one side and principal and surety on other).

6. *See* R. Fleming, PUNISHMENT BEFORE TRIAL 3 (1982) (comparison of widely divergent bail processes in Detroit and Baltimore). When writing a bond, a surety may require the principal to provide collateral in the form of personal property to secure release. *Id.* at 3.

7. *See id.* at 131.

8. *See A Proposal to Modify Existing Procedures Governing the Interstate Rendition of Fugitive Bailees: Hearing on S.2855 Before the Subcomm. on Constitutional Rights and the Subcomm. on Improvement in Judicial Machinery of the Senate Comm. on the Judiciary*, 89th Cong., 2nd Sess. 4 (1966) (statement of Joseph Tydings, Chairman, Subcomm. on Improvements in Judicial Machinery). *See generally The Long Arm, supra* note 4, at 8. *The Long Arm* included a description of the capture, by John Light, a Washington, D.C. bail bondsman, of a principal named Meredith Green. *Id.* at 8. Light traced Green from the District of Columbia to a Maryland apartment. *Id.* at 8. With the help of an agent, Light burst through the door and demanded that Green surrender. *Id.* At this point, Light shot Green, and in the process accidentally shot the agent as well. *Id.* Light claimed

that Green had drawn a gun, but no gun was found. *Id.* Following the shooting, Light dragged Green, in the presence of police, 500 yards across the Maryland District of Columbia state line to where District of Columbia police were waiting. *Id.* Only then was Green taken to a hospital. *Id.*

9. *See, e.g.*, Kear v. Hilton, 699 F.2d 181, 182 (4th Cir. 1983) (professional bondsmen in United States enjoy extraordinary powers to capture and use force to compel return of principal); Allied Fidelity Corp. v. Commissioner, 572 F.2d 1190, 1193 (7th Cir. 1978) (surety has broad powers of custody over principal) *cert. denied*, 439 U.S. 835 (1978); Stuyvesant Ins. Co. v. United States, 410 F.2d 524, 525-27 (8th Cir. 1969) (surety needs no warrant and may go anywhere in United States to arrest principal); Curtis v. Peerless Ins. Co., 299 F. Supp. 429, 435 (D. Minn. 1969) (common law is clear on right of surety to take principal into custody, wherever principal may be, and deliver principal to proper authorities); Livingston v. Browder, 51 Ala. Ct. App. 366, 368, 285 So. 2d 923, 925 (Ct. Civ. App. 1973) (bondsman may exercise great discretion in arresting principal).

10. 76 U.S. (9 Wall.) 13 (1869) (Court held that United States could not recover against sureties who had not produced principal when government had consented to principal's travels beyond reach of sureties).

11. *Id.* at 14.

12. *Id.* at 15.

13. *Id.* at 16.

14. *Id.* at 22.

15. *Id.* at 21-22. The *Reese* Court distinguished the liabilities of a surety on a personal recognizance from a surety on an ordinary bond or commercial contract. *Id.* at 21. According to the Court, the surety on a personal recognizance may discharge himself on the contract at any time by surrendering the principal to the court issuing the bond. *Id.* The death of the principal also discharges the surety. *Id.* A surety on an ordinary bond or commercial contract is liable until payment of the debt or performance of the stipulated act. *Id.* The precise terms of the contract, however, limit liability for both types of sureties. *Id.*

16. *See id.* at 21 (surety may not subject principal to constant imprisonment).

17. *Id.* at 21-22.

18. 83 U.S. (16 Wall.) 366 (1872). Almost every court hearing a case concerning the extraordinary arrest powers and authority of sureties cites or quotes *Taylor v. Taintor*. *See, e.g.*, Kear V. Hilton, 699 F.2d 181, 182 (4th Cir. 1983) (citing *Taylor* as source for extraordinary powers of sureties); Allied Fidelity Corp. v. Commissioner, 572 F.2d 1190, 1193 (7th Cir. 1978) (citing *Taylor* as basis for broad powers of surety) *cert. denied*, 439 U.S. 835 (1978); Maynard v. Kear, 474 F. Supp. 794, 803 (N.D. Ohio 1979) (quoting *Taylor* as settling issue of common-law right of recapture by surety); Citizens for Pre-Trial

Justice v. Goldfarb, 88 Mich. App. 519, 565, 278 N.W.2d 653, 676 (1979) (quoting *Taylor* for court approval of common-law authority of bondsman to arrest and surrender principal) (Brennan, J., concurring in part and dissenting in part), *modified*, 327 N.W.2d 910 (1982).

19. *Taylor*, 83 U.S. at 368-69.

20. *Id.* at 368.

21. *Id.*

22. *Id.*

23. *Id.* at 368-69.

24. *Id.* at 371-75.

25. *See id.* at 369-75.

26. *Id.* at 371. The Supreme Court in *Taylor v. Taintor* specified certain arrest powers of sureties. *Id.* The *Taylor* Court stated that sureties may arrest and deliver a principal at any time and arrest a principal in any state. *Id.* Additionally, the *Taylor* Court stated that sureties may act in person or hire agents. *Id.* Furthermore, the Court stated that under common law, sureties may imprison a principal until delivery is possible. *Id.* Finally, the Court acknowledged that sureties have the authority to break and enter into a principal's house for the purpose of arresting the principal. *Id.*

27. 46 F.2d 40 (5th Cir. 1931).

28. *Id.* at 40.

29. *Id.*

30. *Id.*

31. *Id.*

32. *Id.*

33. *Id.*

34. *Id.* at 41-42.

35. *See id.* at 40-42 (discussion of powers of sureties as arising from private contract).

36. *Id.* at 40.

37. *Id.* at 40. In *Fitzpatrick v. Williams*, the United States Court of Appeals for the Fifth Circuit found no conflict between the interests of the state and interests of the bondsman. *Id.* at 40-41. The Fifth Circuit also stated that the right of the surety to recapture the principal was a private, not a governmental, remedy. *Id.* at 40. Furthermore, the *Fitzpatrick* court held that although the surety may arrest and surrender the principal before the bond is due, the state could not. *Id.* at 41. The Fifth Circuit, therefore, noted that since the state had no right of discretionary rearrest and removal, the surety could not acquire the right to arrest through subrogation. *Id.* at 42. The *Fitzpatrick* court held that the right to arrest was an original right arising from the relationship between the principal and the surety. *Id.* Additionally, the *Fitzpatrick* court indicated that the acquisition of rights through subrogation distinguished a civil surety from a surety on recognizance. *Id.* at 41; *see supra* note 15 (discussion by *Reese* Court of difference between surety on personal recognizance and surety on commercial contract).

38. *See Fitzpatrick*, 46 F.2d at 41.

39. *See e.g.*, Stuyvesant Ins. Co. v. United States, 410 F.2d 524, 525 (8th Cir. 1969) (court cited *Reese* as support for authority of bondsman to arrest principal anywhere in United States without warrant); Curtis v. Peerless Ins. Co., 299 F. Supp. 429, 435 (D. Minn. 1969) (court cited *Taylor* and *Fitzpatrick* as support for authority of bondsman to recapture principal without risking liability to principal); Thomas v. Miller. 282 F. Supp. 571, 573 (E.D. Tenn. 1968) (court cited *Taylor* and *Fitzpatrick* as support for authority of surety to arrest and remove principal from Ohio to Tennessee); Citizens for Pre-Trial Justice v. Goldfarb, 88 Mich. App. 519, 565-66, 278 N.W.2d 653, 674 (1979) (court cited *Taylor* and *Fitzpatrick* as support for constitutionality of Michigan statute codifying common-law rights and liabilities of sureties on bail bond contract, *modified* 327 N.W.2d 910 (1982); *see also* Taylor v. Taintor, 83 U.S. (16 Wall.) 366, 371 (1872) (Court stated common law powers of sureties to arrest and deliver principals); Reese v. United States, 76 U.S. (9 Wall.) 13, 21-22 (1869) (Court discussed almost unlimited authority of sureties over principals); Fitzpatrick v. Williams, 46 F.2d 40, 40-42 (5th Cir. 1931) (court affirmed *Taylor* common-law principles under private contract analysis); *supra* notes 15-17 and accompanying text (discussion of *Reese* decision concerning authority of sureties); *supra* notes 24-26 and accompanying text (discussion of *Taylor* concerning authority of sureties); *supra* notes 35-37 and accompanying text (discussion of *Fitzpatrick* decision concerning common-law powers of sureties).

40. *See generally*, Hansen, *The Professional Bondsman: A State Action Analysis*, 30 Clev. St. L. Rev. 595, 604-09, 621-26 (1981) (survey of state statutes regulating bonding process).

41. *See* Ill. Rev. Stat. ch. 38, § 110-1 to § 110-17 (1980) (statute permits ten percent deposit bail exclusive of corporate bail); Ky. Rev. Stat. § 431-510 (Baldwin 1976) (practice of issuing corporate bond is criminal offense); Or. Rev. Stat. §§ 134.255, 135.260 and 135.265 (1979) (pretrial release permitted only through personal recognizance, supervised or conditional release, and ten percent deposit bonds).

42. *See generally* Hansen, *supra* note 40, at 621-26. Connecticut requires a surety to verify under oath that a principal intends to escape before issuing an arrest warrant. Conn. Gen. Stat. §§ 54-56, 52-319 (West 1978). Moreover, only law enforcement personnel in Connecticut may arrest principals. *Id.* § 52-319 (West 1978). In Texas, sureties may arrest principals only after obtaining arrest warrants from the judiciary. Tex. Code Crim. Proc. Ann. art. 17.19 (Vernon 1977). Many states require sureties to obtain written authority endorsed on a certified copy of the bond, or bail piece, before arresting principals. *See, e.g.*, Ala. Code § 15-13-62 (1975); Ark. Stat. Ann. § 43-717 (1977); Cal. Penal Code § 1301 (West 1982); Idaho Code § 19-2925 (1979); Mo. Ann Stat. § 544.600 (Vernon 1949); Mont. Code Ann. § 46-9-205 (1984); Ohio Rev. Code Ann. § 2713.22 (Baldwin 1982); Okla Stat. Ann. tit. 22 § 1107 (West 1951); Tenn. Code Ann. § 40-11-133 (1982); Utah

Code Ann. § 77-43-23 (1982); Va. Code § 19.2-149 (1950); Wisc. Stat. Ann. § 818.21 (West 1977). Alabama, Nevada, Tennessee, Missouri and Oklahoma have enacted statutes permitting sureties to arrest principals only within the jurisdiction of the state. See Ala. Code § 15-13-63 (1975); Mo. Ann. Stat. § 544.600 (Vernon 1949); Nev. Rev. Stat. § 178.526 (1979); Okla. Stat. Ann. tit. 22, § 1107 (West 1951); Tenn. Code Ann. § 40-11-133 (1982). California requires California sureties to surrender a principal within forty-eight hours after the arrest. Cal. Penal Code § 1301 (West 1982); *see also* Cal. Penal Code § 847.5 (West 1970) (statute regulating surety arrests by foreign bondsmen).

Section 847.5 of the California Penal Code abrogates the foreign bondsman's common-law right to recapture and remove a principal from California. *Id.* The bondsman must file an affidavit with a magistrate in the California county where the fugitive is present, stating the name and location of the fugitive, the offense charged and other particulars. *Id.* If the magistrate concludes that probable cause exists for believing that the person alleged to be the fugitive is such, the magistrate may issue an arrest warrant. *Id.* Any arrest made, therefore, is upon authority of the warrant. *Id.* Following the arrest, the magistrate must hold an additional hearing at which the principal may have counsel. *Id.* After the hearing, if satisfied with the evidence, the magistrate may issue an order permitting the bondsman to return the fugitive to the court from which the fugitive escaped bail. *Id.* Any arrest not made pursuant to the statute is a misdemeanor offense. *Id.; see* Ouzts v. Maryland Nat'l Ins. Co., 505 F.2d 547, 552-55 (9th Cir. 1974) (en banc) (interpretation of § 847.5 of California Penal Code), *cert. denied*, 421 U.S. 949 (1975). In *Ouzts v. Maryland Nat'l Ins. Co.*, Las Vegas police arrested and charged Ouzts with obtaining money under false pretenses in October, 1965. *Id.* at 549. The Justice Court for the Township of Las Vegas set bail at $2,500. *Id.*

Defendant Embrey, agent for the bonding company, posted bond. *Id.* Darrow and Iola Peterseon executed the agreement as indemnitors. *Id.* Ouzts left Nevada and eventually resided in Long Beach, California. *Id.* The Petersons travelled to California and unsuccessfully attempted to arrest Ouzts on November 3, 1966, contrary to § 847.5 of the California Code. *Id.; see* Cal. Penal Code § 847.5 (West 1970) (provisions requires foreign surety to obtain arrest warrant). The Petersons then attempted to comply with the California Code by obtaining an arrest warrant. 505 F.2d at 549. Finally on November 18, 1966, the Petersons hired another agent, W. I. Lagatella, to take Ouzts into custody and deliver Ouzts to Las Vegas. *Id.* Lagatella and an associate arrested and delivered Ouzts to Embrey and the Petersons in San Pedro. *Id.* at 550. The arrest of Ouzts allegedly involved the use of force. *Id.* at 550. The Petersons and Embrey delivered Ouzts to Las Vegas. *Id.* at 550. The police jailed Ouzts from November 18 to November 29, 1966. *Id.* at 556 (Hufstedler, J. dissenting). On January 6, 1967, the

Justice Court for the Township of Las Vegas dismissed the criminal complaint against Ouzts without a hearing. *Id.* The United States Court of Appeals for the Ninth Circuit held that the bondsman completely violated, not merely exceeded, the authority granted to sureties by the California statute. *Id.* at 554. According to the Ninth Circuit, § 847.5 completely terminates a foreign bondsman's common-law recapture right. *Id.*

43. *See supra* notes 24-26 and accompanying text (discussion of common law powers of sureties); Citizens for Pre-Trial Justice v. Goldfarb, 88 Mich. App. 519, 564-67, 278 N.W.2d 653, 676-77 (1979) (court held Michigan statue codifying common-law powers of sureties constitutional), *modified* 327 N.W.2d 910 (1982). In *Citizens for Pre-Trial Justice v. Goldfarb*, the Court of Appeals of Michigan contended, in dicta, that Michigan Comp. Laws § 765.26 regulating the activities of the bail bondsmen was unconstitutional. *Id.* at 551-61, 278 N.W.2d at 668-74; *see also* Mich. Comp. Laws § 765.26 (1982) (regulation of activities of bail bondsman). The *Goldfarb* court contended that the statute was an unconstitutional grant of an arrest power in violation of the due process clauses of the state and federal constitutions. *Goldfarb*, *Id.* at 551, 278 N.W.2d at 668. According to the *Goldfarb* court, the Michigan statute did not require a surety to articulate reasons for revocation of a bail bond, or establish standards defining permissible circumstances for revocation. *Id.* at 552, 278 N.W.2d at 668. Additionally the *Goldfarb* court contended, in dicta, that the statute was unconstitutional because the statue failed to require the procedural safeguards applicable to civil arrests in violation of the fourteenth amendment to the United States Constitution. *Id.* at 556, 278 N.W.2d at 670. The dissent, however, concurred with the majority opinion, except for the portion holding the statute unconstitutional. *Id.* at 564, 278 N.W.2d at 674 (Brennan, J., concurring in part, dissenting in part). The dissent stated that the pertinent statute represented the State of Michigan's return to the common-law rights and liabilities of sureties on a bail bond contract. *Id.* at 556, 278 N.W.2d at 674. Because the dissent constituted a majority of the three judge panel, the Michigan statute regulating bail bond practices was constitutional. *Id.* at 567, 278 N.W.2d at 675.

44. *See* Hansen, *supra* note 40, at 623 (survey of state statutes regulating bonding process).

45. *See, e.g.*, Dunkin v. Lamb, 500 F. Supp. 184, 188 (D. Nev. 1980) (bondsmen beat principal in presence of police at police station); Maynard v. Kear, 474 F. Supp. 794, 799 (N.D. Ohio 1979) (bondsmen seized, beat and dragged principal clad only in underwear from apartment at night in January); Hill v. Toll, 320 F. Supp. 185, 186 (E.D. Pa. 1970) (bail bonding agents allegedly beat and robbed principal at detention center in presence of detention center officials); Thomas v. Miller, 282 F. Supp. 571, 572 (E.D. Tenn. 1968) (bondsman allegedly forced chained and handcuffed principal to lie on the floor of car during trip from Ohio to Tennessee); McCaleb v. Peerless Ins. Co.,

250 F. Supp. 512, 513-15 (D. Neb. 1965) (bondsman seized and held principal for eighty hours while demanding money from principal's parents and unspecified others); United States v. Trunko, 189 F. Supp. 559, 565 (E.D. Ark. 1960) (court characterized treatment of principal by bondsman as unreasonable, high-handed and oppressive); Nicolls v. Ingersoll, 7 Johns. 145, 147-8 (N.Y. 1810) (bondsman used "great roughness" in arresting principal); State v. Lingerfelt, 14 S.E. 75, 75 (N.C. 1891) (bondsman and agent shot and killed principal); Poteete v. Olive, Tenn., 527 S.W.2d 84, 86 (Tenn. 1975) (bondsman broke principal's leg).

46. *See* United States v. Trunko, 189 F. Supp. 559, 561-62 (E.D. Ark. 1960) (method of surety arrest excited and upset principal's wife); Mease v. State, 165 Ga. App. 746, 747-50, 302 S.E.2d 429, 430-31 (1983) (drunken bondsmen using abusive language and waving pistol forced way into home of principal's mother). *Mease v. State* involved a criminal trespass charge that the State of Georgia brought against two licensed female bondsmen. *Mease*, 165 Ga. App. at 747, 302 S.E.2d at 430. After drinking at six different bars during the night, bondsmen Mease and Burke arrived at the home of the principal's mother at 5:00 a.m. *Id.* at 749, 302 S.E.2d at 432 (Deen, J., dissenting). After pounding on the door and gaining entry, the bondsmen conducted a fruitless search of the mother's house without permission. *Id.* at 747, 302 S.E.2d at 430. The conduct of the bondsmen during the search included the use of profanity and obscene language, belligerent attitudes, and the pointing and waving of a pistol. *Id.* at 747-78, 302 S.E.2d at 430-31. The bondsmen continued the search despite the mother's insistence that the principal was not there and despite the mother's demands that the bondsmen leave. *Id.* at 750, 302 S.E.2d at 432 (Deen, J. dissenting). The Court of Appeals of the State of Georgia held that the bondsmen were not guilty of criminal trespass because the bondsmen had entered the house for a lawful reason. *Id.* at 747-48, 302 S.E.2d at 430. Additionally, the *Mease* court held that bondsman Mease was not guilty of reckless conduct, but did affirm Mease's misdemeanor convictions of pointing a pistol at another. *Id.* at 718-49, 302 S.E.2d at 431. The dissent contended that the legal right to arrest one person does not include the right to run rampant through a third party's home in violation of the third party's constitutional rights. *Id.* at 749, 302 S.E.2d at 433 (Deen, J., dissenting).

47. *See* Poteete v. Olive, 527 S.W.2d 84, 88 (Tenn. 1975); *see also infra* notes 48-59 and accompanying text (discussion of *McCaleb v. Peerless*). In *Poteete v. Olive*, a bondsman's agents beat and kicked a principal and broke the principal's leg while making an arrest. *Poteete*, 527 S.W.2d at 86. The principal wore a series of casts for two months and required crutches for four more months. *Id.* The principal sued for false imprisonment, assault and battery. *Id.* at 85. The Tennessee Supreme Court decided the case on the narrow grounds that the arrest was illegal because the agents had violated a Tennessee statute by not obtaining and displaying a certified copy of the endorsed bond.

Id. at 88; *see* Tenn. Code Ann. § 40-1 (1982) (copy of an endorsed bond substitutes for a warrant).

48. 250 F. Supp. 512 (D. Neb. 1965).

49. *Id.* at 513. (Plaintiff alleged violation of liberties under Title 42 U.S.C. § 1983, but court did not address § 1983 claim.)

50. *Id.* at 514.

51. *Id.*

52. *Id.*

53. *Id.*

54. *Id.*

55. *Id.* (court also noted that Vinci fed McCaleb during return trip to Omaha and released McCaleb from shackles).

56. *Id.*

57. *Id.* at 514-15.

58. *Id.* at 515.

59. *Id.*

60. *See* Note, *The Hunters and the Hunted: Rights and Liabilities of Bailbondsmen*, 6 Fordham Urb. L.J. 333, 342 (1978) (examination of bail bondsman's arrest power and various remedies through tort and civil rights suits).

61. *McCaleb*, 250 F. Supp. at 515. In *McCaleb v. Peerless Ins. Co.*, the principal received $4000 in damages from the bonding company for the value of McCaleb's automobile and for illegal imprisonment. *Id.* at 516.

62. *See* 42 U.S.C. § 1983 (1982) (person acting under color of any statute, ordinance, regulation, custom or usage, of any state, who deprives another of any right, privilege or immunity secured by United States Constitution, is liable in action at law); *infra* notes 97-104 and accompanying text (discussion of § 1983 requirements and relationship between "color of state law" and "state action" requirements); *infra* notes 67-96 and accompanying text (discussion of cases challenging the authority and practices of bail bondsmen under § 1983).

63. *See supra* note 62 (text of § 1983).

64. *See* 42 U.S.C. § 1983 (1982) (statute provides remedy for deprivation of constitutional or legal right by person acting under color of state law). Several courts have analyzed the elements necessary to establish a principal's claim under § 1983. *See, e.g.*, Ouzts v. Maryland Nat'l Ins. Co., 505 F.2d 547, 550 (9th Cir. 1974); Maynard v. Kear, 474 F. Supp. 794, 797 (N.D. Ohio 1979); Smith v. Rosenbaum, 333 F. Supp. 35, 38 (E.D, Pa. 1971) *aff'd*, 460 F.2d 1019 (1972); Hill v. Toll, 320 F. Supp. 185, 186 (E.D. Pa. 1970) *See generally* Note, *The Supreme Court Corrals A Runaway Section 1983*, 34 Mercer L. Rev. 1073, 1074-83 (1983) (discussion of history of § 1983 and threshold requisites).

65. *See supra* note 64 (cases discussing elements of claim under § 1983).

66. *See infra* notes 67-79 and accompanying text (discussion of federal court decisions holding that bondsmen acted under color of

state law).

67. 189 F. Supp. 559 (E.D. Ark. 1960), In *United States v. Trunko*, the principal, Williams, owed a fee of $50 to the bonding company for a $500 bond posted on a charge of driving while intoxicated. *Id.* at 560. Williams left Ohio and returned to the Arkansas home of Williams' father. *Id.* The bonding company sent a special investigator, Trunko, to locate Williams. *Id.* at 560-61. Trunko and a companion, Pratt, arrived at the father's home before daylight. *Id.* at 581. Trunko and Pratt entered the house, and without knocking, entered the room where Williams, his wife and infant child were asleep. *Id.* Trunko shone a flashlight into Williams' face and directed Williams to get dressed. *Id.* Trunko handcuffed Williams and drove away at a high rate of speed, seemingly because Williams' wife threatened to call the sheriff. *Id.* at 561-62. Trunko did not advise Williams that Trunko was acting as an agent of the holding company. *Id.* at 562. The family did not know why Williams was arrested. *Id.* Trunko falsely told Williams that they were going to Little Rock, Arkansas. *Id.* Two days later, Williams pleaded guilty to the original charge of driving while intoxicated and the Municipal Court of Ravenna, Ohio fined Williams $250, of which the court would suspend $100 if Williams reimbursed the bondsman. *Id.* The United States District Court for the Eastern District of Arkansas characterized the actions of the bondsmen as high-handed, unreasonable and oppressive. *Id.* at 565.

68. *Id.* at 561.

69. *Id.* at 562.

70. 333 F. Supp. 35 (E.D. Pa. 1971), *aff'd*, 460 F.2d 1019 (1972). In *Smith v. Rosenbaum*, Smith paid Rosenbaum $30 to post a bail bond because of Smith's arrest on a charge of carrying a concealed weapon. *Id.* at 37. Smith also paid bondsman Marks to post bonds for three other arrest charges. *Id.* The charges on the three other arrests included illegal possession of narcotics, carrying a concealed weapon, attempted burglary and possession of burglary tools. *Id.*

71. *See generally* Note, *Bailbondsmen And The Fugitive Accused: The Need For Formal Removal Procedures*, 73 Yale L.J. 1098, 1102 (1964) (defining term "bail piece" as document obtained from court official that is evidence of existence of bond relationship between surety and principal).

72. *Rosenbaum*, 333 F. Supp. at 38. Under Pennsylvania state law, sureties are entitled to a bail piece, issued by the court upon which sureties may arrest and surrender a principal. *See id.; see also* 19 Pa. Stat. Ann. § 53 (1964) (statute entitles sureties to possession of bail piece upon which sureties may arrest principals). The bail piece is sufficient warrant or authority for the sheriff to receive the principal. *Rosenbaum*, 333 F. Supp. at 38. Although the United States District Court for the Eastern District of Pennsylvania in *Smith v. Rosenbaum* held that the act of lodging the bail piece constituted action under color of state law, the principal failed to allege that the bondsmen violated any of the principal's rights, privileges or

immunities secured under the Constitution. *See id.* at 39; *see also infra* note 88 and accompanying text (discussion of principal's constitutional claim).

73. 474 F. Supp. at 794 (N.D. Ohio 1979). In *Maynard v. Kear*, agents of a Virginia bonding company seized and beat Maynard late one January night in Ohio. *Id.* at 799. The agents dragged Maynard, who was clad only in underwear, out of his apartment and handcuffed Maynard in preparation for the trip back to Virginia. *Id.* Maynard's wife called the police, who took Maynard and the bonding agents to the station house. *Id.* at 798-99. Upon advice from the city prosecutor, the police released the bonding agents. *Id.* at 798. During the time the agents were inside the station house, Maynard remained in the agents' car and received no treatment for injuries. *Id.* The police, however, did give Maynard a coat and a pair of pants to wear. *Id.*

74. *Id.* at 800.

75. *Id.* at 801.

76. *Id.*

77. 320 F. Supp. 185 (E.D. Pa. 1970).

78. *See* 19 Pa. Cons. Stat. § 53 (1964) (sureties are entitled to bail piece upon which sureties may arrest and detain principals); *see also supra* note 71 (defining bail piece).

79. *Hill*, 320 F. Supp. at 187. In *Hill v. Toll*, two bonding agents entered the principal's home, and seized and transported the principal to the Philadelphia Detention Center. *Id.* at 186. At the Center, the agents allegedly beat and robbed the principal in the presence of the detention center officials. *Id.*

80. *See, e.g.*, Ouzts v. Maryland Nat'l Ins. Co., 505 F.2d 547, 554 (9th Cir. 1974) (bondsman did not act under color of state law because California statute specifically forbade foreign bondsmen's common-law right of recapture); Thomas v. Miller, 282 F. Supp. 571, 572-73 (E.D. Tenn. 1968) (bondsman's acts were result of private contractual relationship and not under color of state law); *see also* Easley v. Blossom, 394 F. Supp. 343, 345 (S.D. Fla. 1975) (court cited *Thomas* and *Curtis* as support for blanket statement concerning lack of state action in bondsman's actions); Curtis v. Peerless Ins. Co., 299 F. Supp. 429, 431 (D. Minn. 1969) (court dismissed § 1983 complaint because plaintiff failed to sufficiently allege color of state law requirement).

81. *See infra* notes 81-95 and accompanying text (discussion of possible constitutional rights that would meet one of two threshold requirements necessary for § 1983 suit); *see also supra* notes 61-64 and accompanying text (discussion of two elements principal must establish in § 1983 action).

82. *See supra* notes 77-79 and accompanying text (discussion of facts in *Hill* and color of state law element).

83. *See Hill*, 320 F. Supp. at 187.

84. *Id.*

85. *Id.*

86. *Id.*

87. *Rosenbaum*, 333 F. Supp. at 35 (E.D. Pa. 1971); *see supra* notes 70-72 and accompanying text (discussion of facts in *Rosenbaum* and color of state law element).

88. *Rosenbaum*, 333 F. Supp. at 37, 38.

89. *Id.* at 38. In *Smith v. Rosenbaum*, the United States District Court for the Eastern District of Pennsylvania stated that the principal's later arrest, which increased the surety's risk, justified the surety's revocation of the bail bond contract by lodging the bail pieces. *Id.* Additionally, the *Rosenbaum* court stated that the failure of the principal to inform the bondsman of a change of address also justified the revocation of the bond. *Id.* Furthermore, the *Rosenbaum* court noted that the principal had contracted to lose his liberty if the authorities rearrested the principal on another charge. *Id.* at 39. The *Rosenbaum* court addressed the issue of the revocation of the bail bond contract. *Id.* at 37-39. The *Rosenbaum* court did not address the issue of whether procedural requirements are necessary in making a surety arrest because the *Rosenbaum* principal already was incarcerated for a subsequent offense. *Id.* at 37.

90. *Id.* at 39.

91. *See supra* notes 73-76 and accompanying text (discussion of facts in *Maynard* and color of state law requirement).

92. *Maynard*, 474 F. Supp. at 801-04. In *Maynard v. Kear*, the United States District Court for the Northern District of Ohio concluded that by knowingly and purportedly acting under the authority of a state bench warrant, the bondsmen were acting under the color of state law required for a fourteenth amendment and fourth amendment claim. *Id.* at 801.

93. *Id.* at 801-03. In *Maynard v. Kear*, the United States District Court for the Northern District of Ohio stated that all of the protections of the fourth amendment applied with full force to surety arrests with the possible exception of the requirement of an arrest warrant. *Id.* at 802-03. The *Maynard* court focused on the rights guaranteed by the fourth amendment as the most relevant of the constitutional rights that an abused principal has. *Id.* at 801-03.

94. *Id.* at 803; *see* Estelle v. Gamble, 429 U.S. 97, 102-03 (1976) (punishments that are incompatible with evolving societal standards of decency, or which involve unnecessary and wanton infliction of pain, violate eighth amendment).

95. *Maynard*, 474 F. Supp. at 804.

96. *Id.* *See generally* Note, *Interstate Rendition Violations and Section 1983: Locating the Federal Rights of Fugitives*, 50 Fordham L. Rev. 1268, 1268-91 (1982) (discussion of federal and state extradition provisions and requirements for maintaining a section 1983 action). Violations of federal and state extradition provisions by law enforcement officials do not support § 1983 actions because the provisions create no federal rights. *Id.* at 1270-87. Courts should permit § 1983 actions, however, for violation of a fugitive's constitutional right to challenge extradition by writ of habeas corpus. *Id.* at 1287-91; Note,

supra note 71, at 1098-1111 (1964) (discussion of necessity of extending sixth amendment right to full extradition-type hearings to principals).

97. 457 U.S. 922, 923-39 (1982).

98. *See id.* at 923-39 (discussion of relationship between state action requirement of fourteenth amendment and color of state law requirement of § 1983, and analysis of term "state action"). In *Lugar v. Edmondson Oil Co.*, petitioner Lugar was indebted to Edmondson Oil Comapny, which sued on the debt in a Virginia state court. *Id.* at 924. Pursuant to a Virginia state law, Edmondson sought prejudgment attachment of some of Lugar's property. *Id.* Under the state statute Edmondson only had to allege that Lugar was disposing of or might dispose of his property in order to attach the property. *Id.* Because of Edmondson's allegations, the clerk of the state court issued a writ of attachment and the sheriff executed the writ. *Id.* A state trial judge conducted a hearing on the propriety of the attachment, subsequent to the execution of the writ and, thirty-four days after the levy, the judge ordered the attachment dismissed. *Id.* at 925. The state trial judge found that Edmondson had failed to establish statutory grounds for the attachment. *Id.* Lugar sued under § 1983, alleging deprivation of property without due process of law. *Id.* Lugar sought compensatory and punitive damages. *Id.* The United States Court of Appeals for the Fourth Circuit affirmed the trial court's decision that the actions of Edmondson did not constitute state action as required by the fourteenth amendment. *Id.* The Fourth Circuit, therefore, held that Lugar had failed to state a claim upon which a court could grant relief under § 1983. *Id.* On appeal, the United States Supreme Court stated that private misuse of a state statute did not describe conduct fairly attributable to the state *Id.* at 941. The Court held, however, that insofar as Lugar's complaint challenged the constitutionality of the Virginia attachment statute, Lugar had presented a valid cause of action. *Id.* at 942. The Court demonstrated a concern with a statutory scheme in which officials could attach property on the *ex parte* application of one party to a private dispute. *Id.* at 942.

99. U.S. CONST. amend. XIV, § 1.

100. *Lugar*, 457 U.S. at 924.

101. *Id.*

102. *Id.*

103. *Id.* at 935.

104. Note, *supra* note 64, at 1073 (discussion of effect of Lugar and two other recent Supreme Court decisions on § 1983).

105. *Lugar*, 457 U.S. at 937.

106. *Id.*

107. *Id.*

108. *Id.*

109. *Id.* at 939.

110. *Id.* In *Lugar v. Edmondson Oil Co.*, the United States Supreme Court indicated that a court must sift the facts and weigh the

circumstances of each case to determine the true significance of state involvement in private conduct. *Id.*

111. *See* Jackson v. Metropolitan Edison Co., 419 U.S. 345, 353 (1974) (Court applied public function doctrine to only those powers traditionally associated with sovereignty). In *Jackson v. Metropolitan Edison Co.*, a customer of the defendant, Metropolitan Edison, challenged the actions of the privately owned and operated utility corporation as violating due process by terminating service without notice or opportunity to pay outstanding obligations. *Id.* at 347-48. The Court held that the state action was not present because the state had no obligation to furnish utility services and such service was not associated traditionally with sovereignty. *Id.* at 353-54; *see also* Flagg Bros. Inc. v. Brooks, 436 U.S. 149, 157 (1978) (Court limited application of public function doctrine to powers traditionally reserved exclusively to state). *See generally* Hansen, *supra* note 40 at 630-32 (discussion of public function doctrine).

112. *See* Adickes v. S.H. Kress & Co., 398 U.S. 144, 170 (1970) (Court stated that state is responsible for discriminatory act of private party when state, by law, has compelled act). In *Adickes v. S.H. Kress & Co.*, the United States Supreme Court stated that it makes no difference whether a statutory provision, or a custom having the force of law, compels the forbidden act. *Id.* at 171.

113. *See* Burton v. Wilmington Parking Auth., 365 U.S. 715, 722-26 (1960) (discussion of relationship between state and restaurant as indicating existence of state action in conduct of restaurant). In *Burton v. Wilmington Parking Auth.*, a restaurant refused to serve a negro patron. *Id.* at 716. The restaurant was located in a parking building that an agency of the state of Delaware owned and operated. *Id.* The United States Supreme Court held that the state had participated in the discriminatory action of the restaurant because the state was in a position of interdependence with the restaurant. *Id.* at 725. The Court found the interdependent relationship from the mutual conferral of benefits between the agency and the restaurant, from the fact that the restaurant was an integral part of the public building, and from the obligations and responsibilities of the agency for the operation of the restaurant. *Id.* at 724.

114. *See Lugar*, 457 U.S. at 939-41 (discussion of joint activity test in context of prejudgment attachment of property).

115. *Id.* at 941.

116. *Id.*

117. *Id.* at 942.

118. *See supra* notes 105-107 and accompanying text (discussion of two-step procedure in determining presence of state action).

119. *See* Maynard v. Kear, 474 F. Supp. 794, 800 (N.D. Ohio 1979) (bondsmen's actions pursuant to state bench warrant obtained under state statute constituted state action); Smith v. Rosenbaum, 333 F. Supp. 35, 39 (E.D. Pa. 1971) (bondsman's actions pursuant to state statute authorizing bail piece constituted state action), *aff'd*, 460 F.2d

1019 (1972).

120. *See Lugar*, 457 U.S. at 939-41 (discussion of claim involving procedurally defective statute as properly actionable under § 1983 if claimant also meets "state action" element).

121. *See infra* notes 137-43 and accompanying text (discussion of procedural safeguards under fourth and fourteenth amendment applicable to surety arrests).

122. *See Lugar*, 457 U.S. at 942 (due process procedures applicable when state has created system permitting attachment of property on application of one party to a private dispute); *supra* text accompanying notes 115-17 (discussion of necessity for hearing prior to attachment of property on *ex parte* application of one party to private dispute).

123. *See supra* notes 109-14 and accompanying text (discussion of four tests used in determining whether private party is state actor).

124. *See* Citizens for Pre-Trial Justice v. Goldfarb, 88 Mich. App. 519, 556, 278 N.W.2d 653, 670 (1979) (bondsmen exercise arrest power that clearly is adjunct of state's sovereignty), *modified*, 327 N.W.2d 910 (1982); *cf.* Thompson v. McCoy, 425 F. Supp. 407, 409-11 (D.S.C. 1976) (state statute authorizing store security guard to make arrests is grant of police power and arrest is, therefore, under color of state law). *See generally* Hansen, *supra* note 40 at 630-32 (discussion of application of public function doctrine to surety arrests).

125. *See Hansen*, *supra* note 40 at 632-36 (discussion of state compulsion test in context of surety arrest). A demonstration that a statute authorizes and encourages bondsmen to arrest principals will not satisfy the state compulsion test if a bondsman has an alternative means available for surrendering the principal to court. *Id.* at 634. If the state statute permits the surety to employ police officers to aid in the arrest then surety arrest is only one alternative and, therefore, will not meet the compulsion test. *Id.* Courts that have found the conduct of bondsmen to constitute state action pursuant to the compulsion test have reached their conclusion by holding that the bondsmen relied on the state statutes which encouraged or authorized surety arrests. *Id.* at 635; *see* Maynard v. Kear, 474 F. Supp. 794, 801 (N.D. Ohio 1979) (state action lent authority to state to bondsmen); Hill v. Toll, 320 F. Supp. 185, 187 (E.D. Pa. 1970) (state statute encouraged bondsman's conduct).

126. *See* Ouzts v. Maryland Nat'l Ins. Co., 505 F. 2d 547, 555-62 (9th Cir. 1974) (Hufstedler, J., dissenting) (discussion of bondsmen as state actors), *cert. denied*, 421 U.S. 949 (1975). In *Ouzts v. Maryland Nat'l Ins. Co.*, the United States Supreme Court of Appeals for the Ninth Circuit held that a bondsman's conduct did not constitute state action and, therefore, would not support a claim under § 1983. *Id.* at 555, *supra* note 42 (discussion of facts in *Ouzts*). Judge Hufstedler dissented however, stating that the bondsmen were acting under color of state law. *Ouzts*, 505 F.2d at 556. The judge reasoned that substantial governmental cooperation made possible the maintenance of the

system of quasi-private bail ultimately leading to the violation of the principal's civil rights. *Id.* at 557. Judge Hufstedler determined that state action occurred when judicial officers determined eligibility and amounts for bail, imposed bail conditions, and revoked bail ordering recommitments of the principal. *Id.* The judge stated that state action also occurred when state police and judicial officers made the judicial process available to the bondsmen as well as when the state contributed its coercive power to aid in the rearrest and detention of the principal. *Id.* Additionally, Judge Hufstedler believed the state benefitted from the arrangement by saving the expense involved in housing, feeding, clothing and guarding prisoners. *Id.* The judge stated that the fact that the state extensively regulates bondsmen indicated the important public function that bondsmen serve. *Id.* at 559. Judge Hufstedler maintained that the state-licensed and regulated bondsmen are an integral part of the state's program of trial release, and, therefore, the actions of the bondsmen fulfilled the state action requirement. *Id.* In sum, according to the *Ouzts* dissent, state action occurs because of the general governmental nature of the bail system, the comprehensive statutory scheme for licensing and regulating bondsmen, the state's grant to bail bondsmen of police powers not enjoyed by private citizens generally, and the reliance by defendants upon their statutory powers in effecting the arrest of the principal *Id.* at 556; *see also* Citizens for Pre-Trial Justice v. Goldfarb, 88 Mich. App. 519, 557-59, 278 N.W.2d 653, 670-73 (1979) (symbiotic relationship exists between professional bondsmen and state), *modified*, 327 N.W.2d 910 (1982). In *Citizens For Pre-Trial Justice v. Goldfarb*, the Michigan Court of Appeals stated in dicta that a symbiotic relationship between bondsmen and the state indicated that state action existed. *Id.* at 558, 278 N.W.2d at 672-73. According to the *Goldfarb* court, the bondsmen's relationship with a court is quasi-official. *Id.* at 558, 278 N.W.2d at 673. Furthermore, the *Goldfarb* court noted that the state receives benefits from the relationship because the bondsman relieves the state from the burden of caring for the accused. *Id.* at 558, 278 N.W.2d at 673.

127. *See supra* note 126 (discussion of state's regulation of, benefit from and conferral of the arrest power on sureties).

128. *See* Maynard v. Kear, 474 F. Supp. 794, 801 (N.D. Ohio 1979) (joint activity existed when court issued bench warrant pursuant to state statute upon which surety arrested principal); Hill v. Toll, 320 F. Supp. 185, 186-87 (E.D. Pa. 1970) (joint activity existed when court issued bail piece pursuant to state statute upon which surety arrested principal).

129. *See* McCaleb v. Peerless Ins. Co., 250 F. Supp. 512, 514 (D. Neb. 1965) (bondsman lodged principal in various jails during 80-hour trip home); United States v. Trunko, 189 F. Supp. 559, 562 (E.D. Ark. 1960) (court noted bondsman's intention to lodge principal at various jails enroute to jurisdiction of court issuing bond).

130. *See* Mich. Comp. Laws Ann. § 765.26 (West 1982) (provision

entitling surety to assistance of sheriff, chief of police of any city, or any officer in making arrest of principal); *see also* United States v. Roper, 702 F.2d 984, 988-89 (11th Cir. 1983) (court stating that search for fugitives by bail bonding company is service to judicial system, and police assistance in search is reasonable).

131. *See supra* notes 100-104 and accompanying text.

132. *See supra* notes 62-65 and accompanying text (discussion of elements necessary for principal to establish in § 1983 suit).

133. *See* U.S. CONST. amend. XIV. (amendment prohibits states from denying to citizens equal protection of the laws).

134. *See generally* Daykin, *The Constitutional Doctrine of Incorporation Re-Examined*, 5 U.S.F.L. Rev. 61, 61-63 (1970) (discussion of incorporation doctrine through analysis of United States Supreme Court cases applying provisions of first eight amendments to states through fourteenth amendment); *see also* Frankfurter, *Memorandum on "Incorporation" of the Bill of Rights Into the Due Process Clause of the Fourteenth Amendment*, 78 Harv. L. Rev. 746, 746-83 (1965) (collection of cases rejecting claims that certain provisions of first eight amendments to constitution apply to states through incorporation under fourteenth amendment).

135. *See* Benton v. Maryland, 395 U.S. 784, 793-796 (1969) (court held that fifth amendment prohibition against double jeopardy is fundamental right and should apply to states through fourteenth amendment). The United States Supreme Court in *Benton v. Maryland* rejected the idea that the states could deny basic constitutional rights if the totality of the circumstances did not disclose a denial of fundamental fairness. *Id.* at 795. The Court noted that once the Court decides that a particular Bill of Rights guarantee is fundamental to the American scheme of justice, the same constitutional standards apply against both the state and federal governments. *Id.*

136. *See* Zurcher v. Standard Daily, 436 U.S. 547, 549 (1978) (fourth amendment is applicable to states by virtue of fourteenth amendment); Mapp v. Ohio, 367 U.S. 643, 655 (1961) (fourth amendment rights are enforceable through due process clause of fourteenth amendment).

137. *See* Maynard v. Kear, 474 F. Supp. 794, 801 (N.D. Ohio 1979) (court attempted to define fourth, sixth and eighth amendment rights applicable to arrests by bondsmen).

138. U.S. CONST. amend. IV.

139. *Id.*

140. *See infra* notes 144-58 and accompanying text (discussion of requirement of use of reasonable force and means in context or surety arrest).

141. *See infra* notes 159-82 and accompanying text (discussion of warrant requirements in context of surety arrests).

142. *See infra* notes 184-222 and accompanying text (discussion of notice and opportunity to be heard in hearing in context of surety arrest).

143. *See* Kear v. Hilton, 699 F.2d 181, 182 (4th Cir. 1983) (court noted need for hearing before surety arrest); Maynard v. Kear, 474 F. Supp. 794, 801-03 (N.D. Ohio 1979) (court stated that surety arrests are subject to requirement that arrests may involve use of only reasonable force and means but also stated that surety arrest does not require use of warrants).

144. *See* Costello v. United States, 298 F.2d 99, 100 (9th Cir. 1962) (court held that police used reasonable force in striking accused on head with sidearm when accused charged police officers after announcement of arrest). In *Costello v. United States*, the United States Court of Appeals for the Ninth Circuit affirmed the basic principle that police officers should make arrests peaceably if possible and only forcibly if necessary. *Id.*

145. *See* Moore v. Bishop, 338 F. Supp. 513, 515 (E.D. Tenn. 1972) (accused alleged that police used unnecessary force in subduing accused and unnecessary force after handcuffing accused). The United States District Court for the Eastern District of Tennessee in *Moore v. Bishop* emphasized the duty of a police officer to avoid using unnecessary violence in effecting an arrest. *Id.* Additionally, the *Moore* court emphasized that an officer may not use force or violence disproportionate to the extent of the resistance offered. *Id.* Finally, the *Moore* court indicated that an officer may shoot only when appearances justify a fear of suffering serious injury or loss of life. *Id.*

146. *See* Curtis v. Peerless Ins. Co., 299 F. Supp. 429, 435 (D. Minn. 1969) (purpose of rearrest by sureties must be proper in light of sureties' undertaking); *accord* Smith v. Rosenbaum, 333 F. Supp. 35, 39 (E.D. Pa. 1971) (court cited *Curtis* as support for nonliability of surety except in cases in which surety has transgressed bounds of reasonable means or improper purpose), *aff'd*, 460 F.2d 1019 (3rd Cir. 1972).

147. *See* Shine v. State, 44 Ala. App. 171, ______, 204 So. 2d 817, 826 (1967) (discussion of use of force in surety's arrest of principal). In *Shine v. State* the Alabama Court of Appeals stated that a court should reexamine the means used by bondsmen in arresting principals. *Id.* at ______, 204 So.2d at 826. According to the *Shine* court, the "pay or get shot" attitude of bondsmen had continued for too long, and indicated the need for the court to control the bondsmen's use of weapons. *Id.*

148. *Id.* at ______, 204 So.2d at 826.

149. *See* Weissengoff v. Davis, 260 F. 16, 18-19 (4th Cir.) (discussion of use of force by police officer in misdemeanor arrest), *cert. denied*, 250 U.S. 674 (1919); *cf.* Shine v. State, 44 Ala. App. 171, ______, 204 So. 2d 817, 823 (1967) (discussion of use of force in arrest of principal by surety when force resulted in death of surety).

150. *Shine*, 204 So.2d at 823.

151. *See, e.g.*, Curtis v. Peerless Ins. Co., 299 F. Supp. 429, 431 (D. Minn. 1969) (principal's bond was $350 on charge of driving while

intoxicated); McCaleb v. Peerless Ins. Co., 250 F. Supp. 512, 514 (D. Neb. 1965) (principal's bond was worth $200 on charge of violating traffic laws); United States v. Trunko, 189 F. Supp. 559, 560 (E.D. Ark. 1960) (principal's bond was $500 on misdemeanor charge of driving while intoxicated).

152. *See* Ker v. California, 374 U.S. 23, 38 (1963) (discussion of demand-notice requirement in arrest by police officer).

153. *See id.* (demand-notice requirements are not applicable when need to prevent destruction of evidence exists); People v. Maddox, 46 Cal. 2d 301, 306, 294 P.2d 6, 9 (Cal.) (court noted that three exceptions to demand-notice requirement include need to prevent destruction of evidence, increase in peril to officer's life and frustration of arrest), *cert. denied*, 352 U.S. 858 (1956).

154. 4 Conn. 166 (1822).

155. *See id.* at 168 (court limited damages to those actually sustained when bondsman broke door of principal's house).

156. *Id.* at 168. In *Read v. Case*, the Connecticut Supreme Court did not require the surety to give notice of presence and to request entrance because the principal already knew the reason for the surety's presence and because the principal had barricaded and armed himself to defeat the surety's right of recapture. *Id.*

157. *See* Ouzts v. Maryland Nat'l Ins. Co., 505 F.2d 547, 549-50 (9th Cir. 1974) bonding agent hired bounty hunter unknown to principal to take principal into custody), *cert. denied*, 421 U.S. 949 (1975); United States v. Trunko, 189 F. Supp. 559, 562 (E.D. Ark. 1960) (bonding agent Trunko did not advise principal that Trunko was acting as agent of bonding company).

158. *See* United States v. Trunko, 189 F. Supp. 559, 562 (E.D. Ark. 1960) (neither principal Williams nor family knew why bonding agent was arresting Williams).

159. *See infra* notes 160-65 and accompanying text (discussion of warrant requirements in context of arrests by law enforcement personnel).

160. *See* United States v. Watson, 423 U.S. 411, 421-23 (1976). The issue in *United States v. Watson* concerned whether a law enforcement official could make a public arrest for a felony without a warrant but with probable cause. *Id.* at 412-17. According to the facts in *Watson*, a postal inspector had made a warrantless arrest of a suspect based on information that a reliable informant had supplied. *Id.* at 412-13. The trial court held the arrest unconstitutional because the postal inspector had failed to secure an arrest warrant despite ample opportunity to do so. *Id.* at 414. The United States Supreme Court, despite a preference for warranted arrests, held that a warrantless public arrest based on probable cause was constitutional. *Id.* at 423.

161. *See id.* at 423. The Supreme Court in *United States v. Watson* not only considered the strong common-law tradition in holding that warrantless public arrests based on probable cause were constitutional, but the Court also considered congressional preferences. *Id.*

The Court noted that, prior to 1951, Congress had conditioned the warrantless arrest powers of federal law enforcement officials upon the exigent circumstances of the arresting officers' reasonable grounds to believe that the accused would flee if the officers took the time to obtain warrants. *Id.* at 423 n.13. Congress eliminated the condition of exigent circumstances in 1951. *Id.*

162. 445 U.S. 573 (1980).

163. *Id.* at 575. In *Payton v. New York*, six police officers visited Payton's apartment at 7:30 a.m. intending to make a warrantless arrest of Payton for the murder of a gas station attendant two days earlier. *Id.* No one was present, but police seized a .30 caliber shell casing that lay in plain view. *Id.* 576-77. Payton challenged the admission of the casing into evidence at the trial because the officers had failed to seize the evidence properly. *Id.* at 577. The *Payton* Court held that, through the fourteenth amendment, the fourth amendment prohibits state police officers from making a warrantless and nonconsensual entry into a suspect's home to make a routine felony arrest. *Id.* 583-603. Because the search of Payton's apartment was illegal, the United States Supreme Court reversed Payton's conviction and remanded the case to the New York Court of Appeals. *Id.* at 603.

164. *Id.* at 590. The Supreme Court in *Payton v. New York* found persuasive the reasoning that an arrest in a home involves not only the invasion of privacy attendant to all arrests but also an invasion of the sanctity of the home, an invasion which was too substantial to permit without a warrant. *Id.* at 588-89.

165. *See* Steagald v. United States, 451 U.S. 204, 211-16 (1981) (Court compared search for person to search for object in holding that search warrant is necessary before entering home of third party to arrest fugitive).

166. *See* Taylor v. Taintor, 83 U.S. (16 Wall.) 366, 371 (1872) (no arrest warrant necessary in arrest of principal by surety). In *Taylor v. Taintor*, the United States Supreme Court reasoned that a surety did not need to obtain an arrest warrant as the arrest was comparable to the rearrest of an escaping prisoner by a sheriff. *Id.; see supra* notes 18-26 and accompanying text (discussion of *Taylor*).

167. *See* Fitzpatrick v. Williams, 46 F.2d 40, 41 (5th Cir. 1931) (surety does not need process to arrest principal wherever principal may be); *id.* at 40 (surety did not need to obtain arrest warrant because surety was acting upon private contract right of recapture).

168. *See, e.g.*, Maynard v. Kear, 474 F. Supp. 794, 802 (N.D. Ohio 1979) (surety does not need to obtain warrant before arresting principal); Curtis v. Peerless Ins. Co., 299 F. Supp. 429, 435 (D. Minn. 1969) (surety may take principal into custody without legal process); United States v. Trunko, 189 F. Supp. 559, 563 (E.D. Ark. 1960) (surety has right to recapture defaulting principal without resort to extradition or other legal process).

169. *See Maynard*, 474 F. Supp. at 802. In *Maynard v. Kear*, the United States District Court for the Northern District of Ohio discussed

the fourth amendment rights potentially relevant to the bondsman who acts under color of state law. *Id.* In the discussion, the *Maynard* court, while hesitant to require a bondsman to obtain a warrant, did leave open the possibility that under the holding of *United States v. Holmes*, a court might impose a warrant requirement. *Id.; infra* notes 170-74 (discussion of decision by *Holmes'* court that warrantless rearrest by police officers of bailed defendant was not valid).

170. 452 F.2d 249 (7th Cir. 1971), *cert. denied*, 407 U.S. 909 (1972).

171. *See* United States v. Holmes, 452 F.2d 249, 260-61 (7th Cir. 1971), *cert. denied*, 407 U.S. 909 (1972). In *United States v. Holmes*, government agents without a new warrant rearrested defendant Oliver, who was free on bail. *Id.* at 260. The government argued that the return of a new indictment against Oliver established the probable cause necessary to make the rearrest. *Id.* Oliver argued that the warrantless arrest was unconstitutional. *Id.* According to the United States Court of Appeals for the Seventh Circuit, two factors were important in resolving the issue of whether the rearrest was constitutional. *Id.* First, the government must have reason to believe that the prospective arrestee is guilty of a crime. *Id.* Second, the arrest must serve some purpose. *Id.* According to the Seventh Circuit, probable cause existed because the defendant was under indictment. *Id.* at 260-61. The *Holmes* court concluded, however, that the rearrest served no purpose because in the contemplation of the law, the bailed defendant was already in custody. *Id.* at 261. While the *Holmes* court recognized that many valid reasons for rearrest existed, the court concluded that an arrest needed more justification than continuing knowledge of guilt of the offense charged. *Id.* Without more, according to the *Holmes* court, a defendant would be subject to the type of harassment prohibited by the fourth amendment. *Id.* In Oliver's case, if the judge had ordered a change in the defendant's custodial status as a result of the new charges, then the subsequent arrest would have served a purpose. *Id.* The *Holmes* court also noted the fact that the government originally had sought to justify Oliver's arrest on the ground that a warrant had, in fact been issued. *Id.* The government's assertion, however, was in error. *Id.*

172. *Id.* at 261.

173. *Id.*

174. *See id.* at 260-261. One may distinguish the decision in *United States v. Holmes* from a surety rearrest situation in that the United States Court of Appeals for the Seventh Circuit emphasized that the new charge and new warrant were necessary to avoid the harassment of the arrestee by the police. *Id.* at 261; *see also supra* note 171 (discussion of reasoning in *Holmes* decision).

175. *See infra* notes 176-82 and accompanying text (discussion of common law principles applicable to entry into third party dwellings by either sureties or police officers).

176. *Taylor*, 83 U.S. at 371.

177. 51 Al. App. 366, ______, 285 So. 2d 923, 924 (Ala. Civ. App.

1973).

178. *Id.* at _____, 285 So. 2d at 924-25.

179. *Id.* at _____, 285 So.2d at 927. In *Livingston v. Browder*, the Court of Civil Appeals of the State of Alabama emphasized the strong public policy in preventing the principal from leaving the jurisdiction of the bond agreement. *Id.* at _____, 285 So.2d at 925. Additionally, the *Livingston* court noted that, because of this strong public interest, the state permits the surety wide discretion in determining the steps necessary to effect the apprehension of the principal. *Id.* Furthermore, the *Livingston* court stated that the responsibility of the surety to ensure the principal's appearance in court justifies the large amount of authority that the state affords the surety. *Id.*

180. *Id.* at _____, 285 So.2d at 926-27. In discussing the limits of a surety's authority, the Court of Civil Appeals of the State of Alabama in *Livingston v. Browder* compared the arrest of a principal by a surety to the arrest of a suspect by a police officer in discussing the issues of reasonable force and means and warrant requirements. *Id.* at _____, 285 So.2d at 926-27. The *Livingston* court concluded that the law governing the use of reasonable means and force and the lack of necessity for a warrant was the same for a surety as for a policeman. *Id.*at _____, 285, So.2d at 927. In *Livingston*, the surety entered the mother's house when the surety observed the principal leaving through a back alley. *Id.* The presence of these exigent circumstances may explain the *Livingston* court's decision that a warrant was not necessary. *Id.*

181. *Id.* at _____, 285 So.2d at 926-27.

182. *See supra* notes 162-65 and accompanying text (discussion of warrant requirement prior to entry into homes and third party dwellings).

183. *See infra* notes 184-226 and accompanying text (discussion of hearing requirements as applied to different types of arrest and to property attachments).

184. *See* Livingston v. Browder, 51 Ala. App. 336, _____, 285 So.2d 923, 926-27 (1973) (comparison of surety arrest to arrest by police officer).

185. *See infra* notes 197-207 and accompanying text (discussion of right to hearing by parolee or probationer upon revocation of parole or probation).

186. *See infra* notes 209-26 and accompanying text (discussion of right to hearing by private party before attachment of property).

187. *See* United States v. Watson, 423 U.S. 411, 423 (1976) (warrantless public arrest based on law enforcement officer's determination of probable cause is constitutional); *see also supra* notes 160-61 and accompanying text (discussion of circumstances under which warrantless arrests are permissible).

188. *See* Gerstein v. Pugh, 420 U.S. 103, 113-14 (1975) (court struck down Florida statute permitting state to detain person charged by information for substantial period solely on decision of prosecutor).

189. *See id.* at 120 (Court reasoned that informal procedure is justifiable because of lesser consequences, and because it is not critical stage in prosecution).

190. *See id.* at 120.

191. *Id.* at 125.

192. *See* Taylor v. Taintor, 83 U.S. (16 Wall.) 366, 371 (1872) (surety arrest is comparable to rearrest of fugitive by sheriff).

193. *See* Cal. Penal Code § 847.5 (West 1970). California Penal Code § 847.5 totally abrogates the right of a foreign bondsman to pursue, apprehend and remove a principal from California without resort to process that includes hearing. *Id.* The purpose of the first magistrate's hearing, as provided by the statute, is to review the surety's affidavit of facts in support of the surety's request for an arrest warrant. *Id.* Only after a finding of probable cause that the fugitive is present in the county and that the fugitive violated the conditions of bail, will the magistrate issue an arrest warrant. *Id.* Following the arrest, the statute requires an additional evidentiary hearing, with the fugitive present, to establish that the arrestee is the person alleged to have violated bail and that the arrestee is indeed a fugitive from bail. *Id.*

194. *See* Taylor v. Taintor, 83 U.S. (16 Wall.) 336, 371 (1872) (surety may seize principal whenever surety chooses); *see also supra* text accompanying note 193 (discussion of purposes of evidentiary hearing following surety arrest).

195. *See* Gerstein v. Pugh, 420 U.S. 103, 114 (1975) (discussion of purpose of hearing following arrest).

196. *See* Cal. Penal Code § 847.5 (West 1970) (statute requires prompt presentation of principal to magistrate immediately following arrest by surety).

197. *See infra* notes 198-208 and accompanying text (discussion of right to hearing by probationer and parolee upon revocation of probation and parole and analogy to surety revocation of bond); Citizens for Pre-Trial Justice v. Goldfarb, 88 Mich. App. 519, 559, 278 N.W.2d 653, 673 (1979) (comparison of liberty interests of parolee and principal), *modified*, 327 N.W.2d 910 (1982).

198. *See* Morrissey v. Brewer, 408 U.S. 471, 484-87 (1972). In *Morrissey v. Brewer*, the Supreme Court addressed the issue of whether the due process clause of the fourteenth amendment requires a state to afford a parolee an opportunity to be heard prior to revoking parole. *Id.* at 477. In *Morrissey*, the Court heard the appeals of two petitioners. *Id.* at 473. In both instances, the Iowa Board of Parole had revoked the petitioners' paroles without prior hearings. *Id.* The reason given by the Iowa board for revocation of both paroles was the violation of the territorial restrictions placed on the parolees. *Id.* at 473-74. In considering whether due process applied to the parole system, the *Morrissey* Court described the function of parole in the correctional process. *Id.* at 477. The Court described parole practices as an integral party of the penal system, serving as a variation on the imprisonment of convicted criminals. *Id.* According to the *Morrissey* Court, the parole

system alleviates the costs to society of keeping an individual in prison. *Id.* Additionally, the Court noted that in some cases the Board grants parole automatically and in others, parole is a discretionary matter. *Id.* Furthermore, the *Morrissey* Court noted that the state, through the parole board, requires specific restrictive conditions on a parolee. *Id.* The restrictive conditions inhibit the parolee's liberty beyond that of an ordinary citizen, including the stipulation that the parolee remain under the guidance of, and report to, the parole officer. *Id.* at 478. The parole officer generally decides whether to order the revocation of parole. *Id.* at 478-79. The *Morrissey* Court distinguished revocation of parole from criminal prosecution. *Id.* at 480. The agency supervising parole may or may not be acting as an arm of the court. *Id.* Revocation deprives an individual only of a conditional liberty, not the absolute liberty of an ordinary citizen. *Id.* The issue of whether the requirements of due process apply to parole revocations turned on whether the nature of the interest is one within the contemplation of the "liberty or property" language of the fourteenth amendment. *Id.* at 481. The *Morrissey* Court concluded that the liberty, of a parolee, although circumscribed, includes many of the core values of unqualified liberty and the loss of liberty is grievous to the parolee. *Id.* at 482. Since liberty is valuable and is within the protection of the fourteenth amendment, a termination of liberty calls for an orderly process. *Id.*

Principals are in analogous situation to parolees and probationers. The revocation agent, either the surety or the parole officer, may or may not be acting as an arm of the court. *Compare Morrissey,* 408 U.S. at 480 (agency supervising parole may or may not be acting as arm of court) *with* Citizens for Pre-Trial Justice v. Goldfarb, 88 Mich. App. 519, 558, 278 N.W.2d 653, 673 (1979) (bondsman's relationship with court is quasi-official), *modified,* 327 N.W.2d 910 (1982). Both bail and parole are extensions of prison. *Compare Morrissey,* 408 U.S. at 477 (parole is variation of imprisonment) *with* Taylor v. Taintor, 83 U.S. (16 Wall.) 366, 371 (1872) (dominion of surety is continuation of principal's original imprisonment). The position of a parolee and a principal differs only in the requirement of a valid reason to revoke freedom. *Compare Morrissey,* 408 U.S. at 479 (implicit in parole system is idea that parolee is entitled to liberty so long as parolee abides by conditions of parole) *with Taylor,* 83 U.S. (16 Wall.) at 371 (surety may arrest at any time and for any reason).

199. *See* Gagnon v. Scarpelli, 411 U.S. 778, 781 (1973) (decision concerning need for counsel for indigent parolees and probationers is subject to case-by-case analysis).

200. *See* Morrissey v. Brewer, 408 U.S. 471, 480-89 (1972). The United States Supreme Court in *Morrissey v. Brewer* held that a hearing to determine probable cause and to evaluate contested facts was necessary upon revocation of parole. *Id.* at 488. According to the Court, however, the hearing should consist of a narrow inquiry that would be flexible enough to consider evidence not admissible in an adversary criminal trial. *Id.* at 489. The *Morrissey* Court also declined to decide

whether the parolee was entitled to the assistance of retained or appointed counsel. *Id.; see* Gagnon v. Scarpelli, 411 U.S. 778, 781 (1973) (revocation hearing for probationer is subject to same requirements of parolee).

201. *See* Gagnon v. Scarpelli, 411 U.S. 778, 789 (1973) (due process mandates hearing for revocation of probation because loss of significant liberty interests are involved; Morrissey v. Brewer, 408 U.S. 471, 482 (1972) (due process mandates hearing for revocation of parole because loss of significant liberty interests are involved).

202. *See* Morrissey v. Brewer, 408 U.S. 471, 481 (1972) (parolee's right to due process in parole revocation turns on whether nature of parolee's interest is one within contemplation of "liberty or property" language of fourteenth amendment).

203. *See id.* at 482 (parolee's liberty interest is within protection of fourteenth amendment).

204. *See infra* notes 205-08 and accompanying text (discussion of hearing for revocation of bail as differing from hearing for revocation of parole).

205. *See* Morrissey v. Brewer, 408 U.S. 471, 479 (1972).

206. *See* Taylor v. Taintor, 83 U.S. (16 Wall.) 366, 371 (1872).

207. *See* Morrissey v. Brewer, 408 U.S. 471, 487-88 (1972).

208. *See supra* note 193 (discussion of hearing requirements under California Penal Code § 847.5).

209. *See* Kear v. Hilton, 690 F.2d 181, 182 (4th Cir. 1983) (discussion of due process requirements applicable to bondsmen). In *Kear v. Hilton*, Kear a professional bondsman apprehended a principal in Canada and transported the principal to Florida. *Id.* The displeased Canadian officials sought to extradite Kear for kidnapping. *Id.* at 183. The United States Court of Appeals for the Fourth Circuit upheld the lower court's denial of Kear's writ of habeas corpus. *Id.* at 185. The Fourth Circuit stated that a surety's arrest power did not extend beyond the territory of the United States. *Id.* at 182. The Fourth Circuit proceeded on the assumption that the 1872 *Taylor* decision constituted the controlling law. *Id.* at 182 n.2. The Fourth Circuit noted, however, that since 1872, the Supreme Court had imposed procedural due process requirements on the reclamation of property and suggested that these requirements were applicable to the bondsman's situation. *Id.*

210. *See* Fitzpatrick v. Williams, 46 F.2d 40, 40-41 (5th Cir. 1931) (discussion of private contractual nature of bail bond agreement).

211. *See* Hansen, *supra* note 40, at 598 (discussion of typical bail bond contract); *see also* 3 Am. Jur. Legal Forms 2d *Bail and Recognizance* § 35.26 (1971) (provision authorizing surety to arrest and surrender principal at any time in exoneration of surety's liability); 4 Am. Jur. Pl. & Pr. Forms (Rev.) *Bail and Recognizance*, form 91, 92 (1968) (provision authorizing surety to arrest principal).

212. *See* Hansen, *supra* note 40, at 611 (discussion of legality of bail bond contracts).

213. *See* Citizens For Pre-Trial Justice v. Goldfarb, 88 Mich. App. 519, 566, 278 N.W.2d 653, 676 (1979) (court stated essence of bail bond contract is private undertaking), *modified*, 327 N.W.2d 910 (1982). *But cf. supra* notes 81-96 and accompanying text (courts held fourteenth amendment applicable to surety arrest).

214. *See* Lugar v. Edmondson Oil Co., 457 U.S. 922, 941 (1982) (fact that private individual jointly participated with state officials in seizure of disputed property is sufficient to constitute state action under fourteenth amendment).

215. *See id.* at 942 (court focused on state-created system whereby state officials attached property on *ex parte* application of one party to private dispute).

216. 407 U.S. 67, 80-84 (1972) (procedural due process requires opportunity for hearing before state authorizes agents to seize property in possession of person upon application of another).

217. *Id.* at 69-70. In *Fuentes v. Shevin*, the contract in issue was a printed form sales contract that included provisions for seller's repossession of the merchandise on buyer's default. *Id.* at 94. The terms of the contract appeared in small type without accompanying clarifications. *Id.*

218. *See id.* at 73-78; *see also* Fla. Stat. Ann. § 78.01 (Supp. 1972-1973) (amended 1973) (statute permits any person whose goods are wrongfully detained to have writ of replevin); Fla. Stat. Ann. § 78.07 (Supp. 1972-1973) (repealed 1973) (statute requires creditor to post bond payable to defendant if defendant recovers judgment); Pa. Stat. Ann., Tit. 12, § 1821 (1967) (statute authorizes writ of replevin for prejudgment attachment of property).

219. *Fuentes*, 407 U.S. at 69.

220. *Id.* at 80-93.

221. *Id.* at 80-84.

222. *See infra* notes 223-26 and accompanying text (discussion of similarities in attachment of interests by one party in a private contract dispute, whether party is creditor or bondsman).

223. *See* Owenbey v. Morgan, 256 U.S. 94, 110 (1921) (due process clause of fourteenth amendment restrains state action and requires hearing whether liberty or property is at stake).

224. *Id.*

225. *See* Citizens For Pre-Trial Justice v. Goldfarb, 88 Mich. App. 519, 559, 278 N.W.2d 653, 673-74 (1979) (person released on bail bond contract enjoys core values of liberty, and fourteenth amendment requires opportunity for hearing), *modified*, 327 N.W.2d 910 (1982).

226. *See Fuentes*, 407 U.S. at 84 (right to a hearing attaches to deprivation of interest encompassed within the fourteenth amendment's protection). According to *Fuentes v. Shevin*, the United States Supreme Court has permitted summary seizure of property only to collect the internal revenue of the United States, to meet the needs of a national war effort, to protect against the economic disaster of a bank failure, and to protect the public from misbranded drugs and

contaminated food. *Id.* at 91-92.

227. *See supra* notes 9-39 and accompanying text (discussion of broad common-law grant of authority to bondsmen).

228. *See supra* notes 40-44 and accompanying text (discussion of state statutes regulating and licensing bondsmen).

229. *See supra* notes 45-61 and accompanying text (discussion of surety abuse of principals and reaction of courts under basic tort law).

230. *See supra* notes 62-96 and accompanying text (discussion of cases challenging bail bond practices under § 1983).

231. *See supra* notes 62-65 and accompanying text (discussion of elements necessary in § 1983 claim); *supra* notes 97-131 and accompanying text (discussion of requirements necessary to meet the state action element); *supra* notes 132-226 (discussion of approaches applicable to deprivation of constitutional right requirements).

232. *See supra* notes 115-17, 209-26 and accompanying text (application of specific *Lugar* approach and analysis under fourteenth amendment).

233. *See supra* notes 118-31 and accompanying text (discussion of state action requirements).

234. *See supra* notes 132-208 and accompanying text (discussion of fourth and fourteenth amendment protections actionable under § 1983).

APPENDIX D

Forms

Before using the following forms, they should be checked for legality in your area of operations — state, county, and city.

You may want to take them to a typesetter and have them personalized by adding or deleting information and/or including your name and address.

You can also make master photocopies directly from this book using any copier set on the "dark" setting, which will make subsequent copies appear better. Use the master copy to make subsequent copies so you won't have to keep bending the book to make them.

ORIGINAL CASE NOTES

INVESTIGATOR: ______________________

CASE: ______________________

DATE	TIME	NOTES

CASE NOTES

For all cases that you work on, you should document the contacts you make, what was said or determined, and the date and time. These notes will be especially useful if the legitimacy of your arrest is later questioned, or if the bondsman wants some evidence that you have indeed worked a case after he's given you a retainer.

AUTHORIZATION OF ARREST OF DEFENDANT ON BAIL BOND

KNOW ALL MEN BY THESE PRESENTS:

That the ______________________ Corporation, does hereby authorize and empower ______________________ as its representative and in its stead, to arrest and detain ____, the defendant in the attached certified copy of bail bond, wherever he may be found in THE UNITED STATES OF AMERICA, and to hold ______________________ in custody and surrender ______________________ to the ______________ court, ______________ city or Judicial District, County of ______________________, State of ______________, wherein proceedings against said defendant described in said bail bond are now pending.

Dated this ______ day of ____________ 19 ____.
at ______________, ________.

Ins. Co. ______________________

By ______________________
Attorney-In-Fact

AUTHORIZATION TO ARREST

The form presented here may be used as a generic form, if correctly filled out. The name of the surety company should be included in the blank on the first line and in the space provided at lower right (marked "Ins. Co."). A bondsman will help you fill out this form or supply you with one of his own.

Certificate of Surrender of Prisoner By Bondsman

STATE OF ______________________

SHERIFF'S DEPARTMENT
COUNTY OF ______________________ } SS

or

POLICE DEPARTMENT
CITY OF ______________________ } SS

ALLIED FIDELITY INSURANCE CO one of the sureties upon the bail bond of ______________________

______________________, hereinafter called defendant, charged

with ______________________ having

delivered to me a certified copy of the bail bond surrendering said defendant, and I, having thereupon taken in custody the said defendant, do hereby certify and by this certificate acknowledge that ______________________

____

has surrendered the said defendant, and that the said defendant is now in my custody.

Dated ______________________, 19____.

____
Sheriff or Chief of Police

By ______________________
Deputy Sheriff or Jailer

AF-9

CERTIFICATE OF SURRENDER

This form is used when your bondsman or surety company demands a receipt for the prisoner before paying you. Generally, the booking officer at the jail (the officer who takes your prisoner) will sign this willingly. Occasionally an officer will not know what the form means and refuse to sign it. If this happens, politely ask for the watch commander and explain your plight. It helps to have the form completely filled out so the officer won't hesitate to sign, as he might if the form is blank.

INDEMNITOR ORDER OF SURRENDER

DATE: ____________

To: Bail Bond Agent

On the ____________ day of ____________, 19___, the undersigned entered into a bail-bond agreement with you for the execution of a bail bond of the defendant ______________________________ for the amount of $ ______________.

It appearing to the undersigned indemnitor on said bail bond that the above-named defendant is not now a desirable risk and should be surrendered into custody. It is hereby requested that such surrender be effected. The undersigned agrees that the liability on said bail bond shall remain in full force and effect until such time the court having jurisdiction of the case shall exonerate the bail bond and fully release the surety thereon. It is further agreed that any expense incurred by you, including recovery fees, in this transaction of surrender will be reimbursed by the undersigned indemnitor upon demand. It is further agreed that any premium or fee charged by you in connection with this transaction is fully earned and any amount remaining unpaid thereon will be paid by the undersigned upon demand.

In connection herewith, the undersigned hereby agrees to save you harmless from any and all damages that might accrue to you from compliance with this request of surrender of the said defendant.

______________________________ ____________

INDEMNITOR DATE

______________________________ ____________

WITNESS DATE

INDEMNITOR ORDER OF SURRENDER

Oftentimes, the cosigner for the bail has a change of heart and wants the defendant picked up. This occurs when the cosigner hears that the defendant is going to flee the area or has intentions of not making his or her court appearance, which would put the cosigner in a financially precarious position.

This form must be read and signed by the cosigner so he is aware of the recovery costs — your fee — for picking up the defendant.

SANTA BARBARA COUNTY
OFFICE OF
COUNTY CLERK - RECORDER
KENNETH A PETTIT
County Clerk-Recorder
RUTH SCHEPLER
Assistant County Clerk-Recorder
P O Drawer CC
Santa Barbara CA 93102
805/963-7167

EX-OFFICIO CLERK
OF THE
SUPERIOR COURT,
BOARD OF SUPERVISORS,
COUNTY WATER AGENCY,
FLOOD CONTROL & WATER
CONSERVATION DISTRICT,
REGISTRAR OF VOTERS
AND
RECORDER

SUPERIOR COURT OF THE STATE OF CALIFORNIA

FOR THE COUNTY OF SANTA BARBARA

Re: Bail Bond Forfeiture

Gentlemen:

Please take notice that the surety bond posted by you in behalf of the above-named defendant has been ordered forfeited by the Court for failure to appear on the date shown:

NAME	CASE NO.	DATE FORFEITED	BOND NUMBER	AMOUNT

Your contractual obligation to pay this bond will be come absolute on the 181st day following the date of its forfeiture unless the Court shall sooner order the forfeiture set aside and the bond reinstated.

KENNETH A. PETTIT, County Clerk

By:______________________________
Deputy Clerk

CAROL ACQUISTAPACE
Chief Deputy
Registrar of Voters
805/963-7190

MARY LOU MORALES
Chief Deputy
Recorder
805/963-7180

ZANDRA CHOLMONDELEY
Chief Deputy
Clerk of the Board
805/963-7191

ANN WOOTEN
Chief
Superior Court Clerk
805/963-7167

JIM LLAMAS
Chief Deputy, Santa Maria
312 E Cook Street
Santa Maria CA 93454
805/922-7831 Ext 245

LETTER OF FORFEITURE

This is the letter used by the Superior Court of Santa Barbara, California, to notify a bondsman of a bail bond forfeiture. If the fugitive is not found within a specified period of time, the bondsman must pay the posted amount of the bail.

IDENTIFICATION AIDS

As much information as possible should be recorded for each person observed.

Physical Description

Height ____________________

Weight ____________________

Nationality ____________________

Complexion ____________________

Visible Scars ____________________

Tattoos ____________________

Approximate Age ____________________

Build (portly, thin, etc.) ____________________

Facial Hair ____________________

Voice Characteristics (accent, etc.)____________________

Glasses (describe frame and lenses) ____________________

Description of Clothing

Hat or Scarf ____________	color(s)________
Shirt/Blouse ____________	color(s)________
Ties ____________	color(s)________
Jacket/Coat ____________	color(s)________
Belt ____________	color(s)________
Pants/Skirt ____________	color(s)________
Shoes ____________	color(s)________

Additional Information

Vehicle:

Make ____________________

Model ____________________

Color ____________________

License Number ____________________

Direction of travel ____________________

Remarks ____________________

IDENTIFICATION AIDS

This little form is useful for developing an accurate description of the fugitive and the vehicle he or she drives. While used by police for crime reports, you can personalize it to suit your own needs.

WANTED

(YOUR NAME)

Special Bail Bond Investigations

(YOUR PHONE NUMBER AND MAIL ADDRESS)

NAME:

AGE:

BIRTHPLACE:

SIZE:

RACE:

HAIR COLOR:

EYES:

ETC.:

CRIME:

This subject was still at large as of

WANTED POSTER

I use this little gem for situations when I know the defendant is in the area and it's no secret that I'm looking for him or her. The blank areas can be used for photographs, a description of the crime, what to do if one should spot the fugitive, and other data such as the type of car the fugitive drives and the amount of reward (if any).

WATCH COMMANDER'S NOTIFICATION OF BAIL ARREST

FUGITIVE/DEFENDANT ______________________________

D. O. B. ________________ WARRANT NUMBERS

RACE ________________ ________________

____

HEIGHT ________________ ________________

HAIR ________________ NCIC ________________

EYES ________________ FBI ________________

WEIGHT ________________ OTHER ________________

BAIL INVESTIGATORS ______________________________

CAR ________________ LICENSE PLATE # ________________

SUSPECTED LOCATION OR PLACE OF ARREST

____

____

____

____

____

NOTIFICATION OF ARREST

It is a good policy to check in with the local police department in the area you intend to make an arrest. Most police officers will be helpful and courteous. Ask for the watch commander and explain who you are and your intentions. Present to him a filled-out copy of this form. This will placate him and let him know that you intend to make the arrest "by the book."

You will also put the watch commander at ease if your approach is courteous and professional. He has in all likelihood met bounty hunters before and might have had a bad experience. I, for example, go about it this way:

> Good evening, Sgt. Jones. My name is Bob Burton and I'm an investigator for the bail bond industry. I'll be making an arrest at (give the address) and just thought you would like to know what's going on on your streets tonight (handing him the form).

This sort of approach shows respect and professionalism, yet maintains your authority. Remember, you have the legitimate right to make the arrest, assuming you have the correct papers in your possession.

FAILURE TO APPEAR (FTA) WORKSHEET

Subject ______________________________

Aliases ______________________________

1. Bond Amount ______________________________
1. Bond Number ______________________________
2. Bond Amount ______________________________
2. Bond Number ______________________________

Last known address ______________________________

Prior address ______________________________

Place of birth ____________ D.O.B. ____________ Age ______

Hgt. ________ Hair ________ Eyes ________ Wgt. ________

SSN ____________ Dr. Lic.# ____________ State ________

Case # of FTA ________ Court ____________ Jail ________

Charge(s) ______________________________

Arresting Agency ____________ Arresting Officer ________

Prosecuting Attorney ______________________________

Indemnitor of Bond ______________________________

Family/Friends/Coworkers/Contacts **Phone #s**

Spouse ______________________________

Mother ______________________________

Father ______________________________

Brother ______________________________

Sister ______________________________

Friends ______________________________

____

____

FAILURE TO APPEAR WORKSHEET

This simply is a form that might make it easier to get a handle on the data you will have to accumulate for a skip. As you develop as a bounty hunter, so will your own ideas as to what belongs on this worksheet. Use this one as a model and develop your own. Oftentimes the bondsman (or surety company he writes for) will have his own.

LOS ANGELES COUNTY JAIL

BOOKING AND PROPERTY RECORD

	YES	NO
HAVE VD	☐	☐
HAVE HEPATITIS	☐	☐
HAVE TB	☐	☐
EVER HAVE TB	☐	☐

BOOKING NO. | LOC. BKD. | DR. LIC. NO. | STATE 1

JAIL CUSTODY RECORD

ARRESTEE'S NAME (LAST, FIRST, MIDDLE) 2

ADDRESS | CITY | SEX 3

DESCENT | HAIR | EYES | HEIGHT | WEIGHT | BIRTHDATE | AGE 4

VEH. LIC. NO | STATE | RPT. DIST. | AKA/NICKNAME 5

BIRTHPLACE | FILE NO. | AD. CHG 6

AG'Y. OR DETAIL ARRESTING | DATE & TIME ARRESTED | TIME BKD. 7

LOCATION OF ARREST | TOTAL BAIL 8

CHARGE | WARR. COMM. NO. 9

JAIL LOC. | ARRAIGN. DATE | TIME | COURT | PRISONER'S SIGNATURE WHEN BOOKED X 10

SOC. SEC. NO. | OBSERVABLE PHYSICAL ODDITIES | OCCUPATION 11

EMPLOYER (FIRM OR PERSON'S NAME, CITY & PHONE NO.) | SPECIAL MEDICAL PROBLEM 12

CLOTHING WORN | LOCATION OR DISPOSITION OF VEHICLE 13

IN CASE OF EMERGENCY NOTIFY (NAME, RELATIONSHIP, ADDRESS, CITY & PHONE NO.) 14

ARRESTING OFFICER | BOOKING EMPLOYEE | SEARCHING OFFICER | TRANSPORTING OFFICER 15

CASH RETAINED | PROPERTY 16

PRISONER'S SIG., FOR REC'T. OF FOREGOING CASH & PROPERTY X 17

CASH DEPOSITED | PROPERTY 18

19

PRISONER'S SIG. FOR REC'T. OF REMAINING CASH & PROPERTY X 20

76B650C-SH-J-294 5/83

SAMPLE BOOKING SHEET

This sheet, from the Los Angeles County Jail, is fairly representative of most booking sheets. If you are new to the trade, I suggest you make copies of this one and familiarize yourself with the questions by filling it out several times on one of your buddies.

A copy of the booking sheet is often necessary in order to get paid. When booking your man, be sure to get a copy to take back to the bondsman to prove you made the arrest. The bondsman can then use the copy to show the court that the fugitive is in jail, entitling him to exoneration.

CONTRACT FOR APPREHENSION OF BAIL BOND FUGITIVE

This agreement between ______________________ and ______________________ for the purpose of locating and arresting or causing the arrest of ______________________ shall be considered a legally binding contract.

The following conditions apply:

I ______________________ will attempt to locate and arrest the above individual who is currently in violation of a bail-bond agreement that ______________________ is a party to and is a fugitive under the laws of ______________________.

The client ______________________ agrees to pay a fee of $______________ upon return of the fugitive to the jurisdiction from which he/she fled. Or upon effecting the arrest of the fugitive by another agency, the same fee will be due and payable upon demand. The client agrees to pay to ______________________ an initial retainer of $______________. This is nonrefundable and will be credited toward the total arrest fee. The client also agrees to pay all reasonable expenses in addition to the arrest fee. Submission of expenses on a weekly basis will be acceptable to both parties. The agent will keep a daily activity and expense record of which a duplicate will be submitted with the expense billings.

The client will understand that not all bail fugitive investigations result in a successful conclusion. Should this be the case, all fees, expenses, and sums forwarded to the agent will be considered fully earned.

OTHER CONDITIONS:

____

Agent Date

____

Client Date

CONTRACT FOR APPREHENSION

This is the contract I use when the collateral wants to get out of the bail-bond as cosigner. As I mentioned, have it signed in front of a witness, and ask for some money up front.

APPENDIX E

Glossary of Bail Terms

Bail enforcement is a legal affair and as such encompasses all the terminology of the bail bond business and the legal profession in general. The following are some of the more common terms and words you will run into. In many localities you will find unique terms and phrases. It would serve you well to write them down and save them for later reference.

BAIL: The surety or sureties who procure the release of a person under arrest by becoming responsible for his or her appearance at the time and place designated.

BAIL BOND: A written undertaking, executed by the defendant or one or more sureties, stating that the defendant designated in such instrument will, while at liberty as a result of an order fixing bail and of the execution of a bail bond in satisfaction thereof, appear in a designated criminal action or proceeding when his attendance is required, and otherwise render himself amenable to the orders and processes of the court. In the event he fails to do so, the signers of the bond will pay to the court the amount of money in the order fixing bail.

BAIL POINT SYSTEM: A system whereby a predetermined number of points are given for all positive aspects of the defendant's background. The total number of points determines whether the defendant will be released on his own recognizance or the amount of bail to be set for his release.

BAILABLE: Capable of being bailed; admitting of bail; authorizing or requiring bail.

BAILABLE ACTION: An action in which the defendant is entitled to be discharged from arrest only upon giving bond to answer.

BAILABLE OFFENSE: An offense for which the prisoner may be admitted to bail.

BOUNTY: A gratuity, or an unusual or additional benefit conferred upon, or compensation paid to, a person for the capture of a fugitive. "Reward" is more proper in the case of a single service, which can be performed only once, and therefore will be earned only by the person or cooperative persons who succeed in effecting the capture of a fugitive.

CASH BAIL BOND: A sum of money, in the amount designated in an order fixing bail, posted by a defendant or by another person on his behalf with a court order or other authorized public officer, upon condition that such money will be forfeited if the defendant does not comply with the directions of the court requiring his attendance at the criminal action or proceeding or does not otherwise render himself amenable to the orders and processes of the court.

EXONERATION OF BAIL: The release from liability of the sureties on a bail bond either by the surrender of their principal to the proper authorities or by his surrender of himself before the day stipulated in the bond.

OWN RECOGNIZANCE: A release of a prisoner based on his or her local stability, residential stability, and job-related criteria. Often used in lieu of cash or instrument bail. This type of bail denies the bonds agent a role in determining the prisoner's ability to appear in court at the appointed time. Should the "O.R." subject flee, the taxpayer of the local jurisdiction must bear the brunt of a lost bail.

SURETY: One who undertakes to pay money or to do any other act in the event that his principal fails therein. One bound with his principal for the payment of a sum of money or for the performance of some duty or promise and who is entitled to be indemnified by someone who ought to have paid or performed if payment or performance be enforced against him. Everyone who incurs a liability in person or estate for the benefit of another, without sharing in the consideration, stands in the position of a "surety," whatever may be the form of his obligation.

APPENDIX F

Additional Reading

The books listed below dwell on subjects that are too varied and complex to be covered in just one chapter in this book. Paladin Press of Boulder, Colorado, has a most unique and complete catalog of books that will assist you in bail enforcement work. Write them at the address below to get on their mailing list.

Bounty Hunter by Bob Burton. Paladin Press.

Find 'em Fast: A Private Investigator's Workbook by John D. McCann. Paladin Press.

How To Find Anyone Anywhere by Ralph D. Thomas. Thomas Publications.

Shadowing and Surveillance: A Complete Guidebook by Burt Rapp. Loompanics Unlimited.

Undercover Operations: A Manual for the Private Investigator by Kingdon Peter Anderson. Paladin Press.

The following sources offer a complete supply of older books on topics of interest to people in the bail bond industry, and continue to release new titles on pertinent subjects:

Loompanics Unlimited, P.O. Box 1197, Port Townsend, WA 98368.
Paladin Press, P.O. Box 1307, Boulder, CO 80306.
Thomas Publications, P.O. Box 33244, Austin, TX 78764.

About the Author

Considered America's leading (and most feared) bounty hunter, Bob Burton is president of the National Association of Bail Enforcement Agents (NABEA). He has made over 2,700 arrests (sixty percent felons) and is considered by many to be the primary expert and consultant in the field.

Burton is a former U.S. Marine who has served with reconnaissance and intelligence units, both in military and civilian capacities. As a founding member of the Special Operations Association, he served as secretary for three years. Burton is also a founding member of the Force Recon Association and a member of the Association of Federal Investigators.